Integrated Marketing Communications

Integrated Marketing Communications

Don E. Schultz
Northwestern University

Stanley I. Tannenbaum
Northwestern University

Robert F. Lauterborn
University of North Carolina

Printed on recyclable paper

Library of Congress Cataloging-in-Publication Data
Schultz, Don E.
    Integrated marketing communications/Don E. Schultz, Stanley
  I. Tannenbaum, Robert F. Lauterborn.
      p.   cm.
    Includes index.
    ISBN 0-8442-3363-3
    1. Communication in marketing.   I. Tannenbaum, Stanley I.
  II. Lauterborn, Robert F.   III. Title.
  HF5415.123.S38   1992
  658.8'02--dc20   91–44518
                                                            CIP

1995 Printing

Published by NTC Business Books, a division of NTC Publishing Group
4255 West Touhy Avenue
Lincolnwood (Chicago), Illinois 60646–1975, U.S.A.
  4 5 6 7 8 9 BC 9 8 7 6 5 4

Contents

▼

Foreword ix
Preface xi
Introduction xv

1 A History of Integrated Marketing Communications: Why Is It Important Now? 1

World War II   2
The Manufacturing Hero   3
Mass Marketing   5
Demassification   6
Empowerment   8
Future Trends   10
Integration   13

2 How Marketing Communications Works: Or At Least How We Think It Works 17

How Communications Changed   18
Understanding Information Processing   24
Information Processing and Integrated Marketing Communications   38
Replacement or Accumulation? Which Is the Right Model?   40

3 The Basics of Developing an Integrated Marketing Program: How to Get Started 43

Logistics and Communication   44
The New Concept of Marketing Communications   45
Networks and Accumulation Revisited   46
Category and Brand Networks   47
Moving from One-Way to Two-Way Communications   51
Enter the Database   52

The Integrated Marketing Communications Planning
—Model 55
The Circular Nature of Integrated Marketing
Communications 58
Some Additional Examples of the Planning Form 59
The Specifics of Planning 63

4 Strategy Is Everything: Planning the Direction of the Communications Program *64*

You Need a Communication Strategy! 64
A New Way of Thinking 65
The Strategy Is the Thinking Process 65
How to Think through a Strategy 70
The Target Buying Incentive 70
The Product Reality—What's in the Product? 73
Product Perception—What's in the Head? 74
Know Your Competition 75
The Competitive Consumer Benefit 76
The Reason to Believe 78
Tonality/Personality 80
Communication/Action Objectives 81
Perceptual Change 82
Customer Contact Points 83
The Future 84

5 From Strategy to Creative Execution: Capturing the Imagination *87*

The Creative Process 87
The Creative Person 88
The Selling Idea 89
Where Does the Selling Idea Come From? 91
Don't Settle for Less than a Good Idea 96

6 Compensation: How Much for Doing What? *99*

Incentive Systems 101
Other Compensation Systems 102

7 Measurement: What Did We Really Get from All the Time, Work, and Money We Invested? *107*

Database Analysis   107
Measuring Integrated Marketing Communications   114

8 How to Measure Consumer Responses: Establishing Effective Two-Way Communication *123*

Plan in Advance   123
How to Measure Changes in the Brand Network   125
How to Measure Contacts   132
How to Measure Consumer Commitment   140
How to Measure Customer Purchases   146
Circular Systems   152
The Next Stages of Measurement   154

9 Barriers to Integration: Overcoming the Stumbling Blocks *157*

Why Doesn't Everyone Buy In Immediately?   157
Planning Systems and Marketing Thinking   158
Organizational Structure As a Barrier to IMC   160
Capability, Control, and Commitment   174
Basic Requirements to Overcome the Barriers to IMC   177

10 Two Case Histories: Does Integrated Marketing Communications Really Work? *180*

The American Cancer Society   180
The Milk Carton Case   196

Index *210*

About the Authors *217*

Foreword
by James C. Reilly
IBM Corporation

▼

The practice of integrated marketing communications is emerging as one of the most valuable "magic bullets" companies can use to gain competitive advantage.

Advertising, sales promotion, direct response marketing, and public relations practitioners are busy finding common ground to meet the coming challenge of selling to *customers* rather than *markets*.

Don Schultz, Stan Tannenbaum, and Bob Lauterborn have produced a lively, no-nonsense critique of this fast-moving marketing trend in *Integrated Marketing Communications*.

Taken alone, the early chapters documenting the shift from mass production to mass marketing are worth the price of the book. Yet the real meat of the text is revealed as the authors analyze the emerging reality of true one-on-one marketing to *individuals*; a reality made possible by the power of information technology to develop this ultimate consumer segmentation approach.

Indeed, the growing worldwide networks created by computer and communications technology have produced stunning changes in how businesses, governments, and individuals work. The extraordinary power of information to break down corporate, geographic, and political borders enables marketing to reach into homes and offices in a matter of weeks or days.

Treating information as a defining element of business strategy, the authors believe the critical issue for most marketers is their ability to control the information consumers use to form and adjust their attitudes, especially as most consumers do not differentiate among the sources of information. The antidote: Manage the flow through integration.

Yet, integration can be a limiting concept if it focuses on media choice and execution alone. Seamless communications must be built on outstanding marketing strategy and thinking. There is no point in speaking with one voice if the message makes no sense!

Schultz, Tannenbaum, and Lauterborn, make their most intriguing case in asserting that many companies are held hostage to traditional marketing variables such as product development, price, or distribution. "What most marketers face today is a parity marketplace," they say, "in which the only true differentiating features are either logistics or communications."

One might also add that companies now face sophisticated consumers who are no longer content to be at the end of a marketing food chain that starts with the premise: "We make, you take," or "We speak, you listen." Moreover, as the center of innovation shifts from the laboratory to the customer so, too, will a company's marketing be defined by the customers' agenda. In such an environment, the premium will be placed more on the relationship and less on the transaction.

Because of that, and in view of their opinions on the erosion of traditional marketing concepts, the authors boldly predict that once logistics are mastered it will be integrated marketing communications that will provide "the only sustainable competitive weapon which most marketing organizations will have in the 1990s and into the 21st Century."

I agree.

Preface
by Richard Fizdale
Leo Burnett Company, Inc.

▼

Integrated Marketing Communications could be the most important book on marketing you will ever read. The authors recognize that the mass market is dead. The old assumptions, strategies, and tactics for reaching a broad base of people with a single selling message delivered by mass media are no longer valid. Television, once the greatest mass communications vehicle, is impotent. The database will prove to be a more powerful marketing tool than television *ever* was.

As marketers and advertising agencies grope for solutions in a strange, new world, Schultz, Tannenbaum, and Lauterborn reveal how to plan, coordinate, execute, control, and measure a communications program in the age of information.

New technologies make it possible to segment a faceless populace into a number of clearly different and highly relevant target markets. It is feasible today—and will become more so in the future—to pare a mass down to a single individual. In the United States, with its remarkably diverse population and clearly defined regions, aggregating consumers by gross demographics (as well as the very idea of "mass") was *always* an illusion. The myth endured because we lacked the conceptual framework and tools to break down mass into more sophisticated, accurate, manageable, and profitable segments.

The belief in the existence of a mass market was fostered by two compelling and influential forces: mass production and mass media. The assembly lines and interchangeable parts of the Industrial Revolution produced goods that were more similar than different. People purchased what they could afford and never gave a second thought to their paucity of choices. When Henry Ford declared that his cars came in any color you wanted as long as they were black, nobody balked. They wanted automobiles. To Henry Ford and other manufacturers, the population seemed homogeneous.

Today, when the media tells us cholesterol is bad, we want cholesterol-free food products—or else. Within months, they appear on grocery store shelves. Every product or service category has become increasingly customized. Line extensions offer different features, benefits, and price points to meet the demands of a diversified population. The law of supply and demand may have to be reversed. "Demand and supply" better reflects reality, as consumers gain control over the marketplace.

Mass media existed before television, but after World War II that concept rose to unprecedented heights. With three networks, it was possible to reach virtually everybody with the same message at essentially the same time. Television massified culture, but its power has been fragmented by the proliferation of cable. The viewing audience now chooses from a wide variety of channels that are customized to satisfy a wide range of interests. Network share is declining precipitously. Remote control enables people to switch channels to avoid commercial breaks or to mute the sound on them. People watching a videotaped program can zap commercials, turning the images into a blur and reducing the soundtrack to gibberish. All the time, effort, and money invested in the message is lost.

Compounding the problem is a parallel proliferation of magazines. We can choose from 197 sports magazines, 120 travel magazines, and 93 magazines targeted to automotive buffs. There are even eight publications that address the cemetery management business.

And there has been an avalanche of targeted media, from direct mail to specialized TV shows designed for a doctor's waiting room, to miniature billboards on shopping carts, to billing inserts, to electronic kiosks, to shoelaces that carry messages.

It was easier when three TV networks burrowed into every home. But it was also a waste talking to millions of people who had no interest in a particular category, brand, or selling proposition.

Thankfully, it is now possible for an advertiser to reach every discreet segment with a synchronized multi-media communications program that delivers tailored messages. How to do that effectively and efficiently is the subject of this book.

Integrated Marketing Communications identifies the dynamics of today's marketplace and teaches us how easy it is to prosper under the new rules. Its truths are revolutionary, undeniable, and practical—that's what makes this book important.

Introduction

▼

Integrated marketing communications (IMC). What is it? Who needs it? How do you do it? Is it here to stay? These are some of the questions we'll answer in this book.

We'll also discuss the impact of IMC on the relationship among marketers, agencies, and the media, ranging from altered compensation systems to fundamental reorganizations of all three entities.

Advertising agencies stopped being genuine agencies a long time ago, but what are they now when advertising is not necessarily their lead function? How do the media respond when performance evaluation systems measure them not just on whether they deliver messages, but on sales results in the marketplace? And how can functionally isolated client marketing communications people cross lines and manage efforts that involve cooperation on a scale not manageable by anyone except the CEO or chairman of the board?

Our challenge in providing real-world answers is formidable.

Even a working definition of integrated marketing communications is hard to come by. Asking around produces answers reminiscent of the old blind-man-feeling-parts-of-an-elephant story.

One very large advertiser thinks IMC is just making sure that the message is the same in all the media you use. This may be the elephant's ear.

David Ogilvy thinks IMC means providing "one-stop shopping"—setting up your agency to deliver all the functions a client might want to buy, and learning to manage them together. Maybe this is a tail.

Ogilvy also says that IMC may be the key to getting away from the "disease"of "talking about creativity all the time" and getting back to a focus on sales. This is at least a leg.

Keith Reinhard, chairman and CEO of DDB Needham, sees integrated marketing communications as a way to unleash the creative potential of everyone in the agency, not just writers and art directors. A balancing opinion, and at least another leg.

But agency-side enthusiasm is not universal. A well-known graphic artist describes IMC as "a load of—." Oh, well. Someone has to clean up after the parade's passed by, and this artist may have just described his next job!

Meanwhile, on the media side, pioneer Chris Whittle led the way to a thinking process that began not with a myopic orientation as a publisher or a broadcaster, but as a communication system that understood and could help marketers establish a dialogue with a specific group of potential customers. He even named his fledgling company "13–30"—the age range of the audience he originally invented media to reach. That's the whole hide, and Time-Warner perceptively pulled it over itself when it acquired a substantial interest in Whittle's grown-up company in 1990.

As you will read later, an agency on the West Coast—a Saatchi & Saatchi subsidiary, but obviously independent-minded —donned a similar mantle when it declared that whether or not it had experience in the jewelry or luxury automobile business was less important than the fact that it uniquely understood the mind of the upscale consumer, and that this was how it was redefining its practice. Watch out for that swinging trunk, Madison Avenue.

The elephant's head—the part that must lead—is the client, and here and there even a blind man can feel leadership.

"You don't talk or think like the ad managers we used to call on ten or fifteen years ago,"observed someone to the speakers at a workshop set up to expose publishing company CEO's to the new breed of client marketing communications people.

"That's because we're not like them," responded Xerox's Mary Koelle. "We're business managers who hold significant budget and accountability responsibilities. We think of marketing communications as an integrated functional whole, rather than advertising as a single entity, and we manage for results."

"We're no longer tactically driven, we're strategy-driven," agreed AT&T's Mike Neavill.

"We're no longer the pharmacy where someone comes in to order this or that medicine," added Jim Reilly from IBM. "We're more like doctors—just tell us where it hurts and we'll prescribe everything from a remedy through rehabilitation."

That awful noise you hear is the elephant crashing through the jungle, and a lot of old attitudes, deep-rooted beliefs, and long-standing practices are being crushed, knocked down, and pushed aside.

That's what this book is about.

What is integrated marketing communications? It's a new way of looking at the whole, where once we only saw parts such as advertising, public relations, sales promotion, purchasing, employee communications, and so forth. It's realigning communications to look at it the way the customer sees it—as a flow of information from indistinguishable sources. Professional communicators have always been condescendingly amused that consumers called everything "advertising" or "PR." Now they recognize with concern if not chagrin that that's exactly the point—it is all one thing, at least to the consumer who sees or hears it.

Integrated marketing communications means talking to people who buy or don't buy based on what they see, hear, feel, etc. —and not just about your product or service. It means eliciting a response, not just conducting a monologue. And it means being accountable for results, not just readership scores or day-after recall—delivering a return on investment, not just spending a budget.

IMC is exciting. It's what's happening, and—as agencies, media, and clients alike are realizing—it's not optional.

Read on.

1

A History of Integrated Marketing Communications: Why Is It Important Now?

▼

Peter Drucker makes the point that "Innovation begins with abandonment. It's not what you start, it's what you stop that counts."

It's hard to stop doing what made so many people so much money for so long.

Fifteen years ago, today's 40-year-old marketing and marketing communication managers listened dutifully as their predecessors passed on the lessons they themselves had been taught fifteen years earlier by the first generation of mass marketing professionals.

The marketing catechism written in the '60s grew out of U.S. experience during and after World War II, and it held true for nearly two decades. But then social, political, technological and economic change converged to invalidate the old rules and spin the next generation of managers into "Future Shock," as Alvin Toffler described it.

In his book *The New Realities*, Peter Drucker talks about the existence of "great divides" in history similar to those in geography—points in time after which nothing is as it was before.

Those avid marketing students of the '70s were—even as their mentors spoke—passing through such a time, experiencing the discontinuity we are only now defining. The accumulated wisdom of two decades of business experience was no longer relevant. The maps issued to their guides described a world that no longer existed.

In this chapter we will trace the origin and development of mass marketing, identify the causes of its dissolution, and chart the start of what we now call *integrated marketing communication*, a field that is less an innovation than a response to the fracturing of old rules and reality.

World War II

In the four years following Pearl Harbor, a new business hero was born in America. For decades, the figures of business legend had been the larger-than-life financiers and empire builders, the risk takers and visionaries—the Morgans, Rockefellers, Carnegies, and Flaglers. In the 1920s and '30s popular imagination began to embrace individuality, engineering, and a new design sense. Look at the cars and kitchens of the time, and the structures designed by Frank Lloyd Wright in real life and Howard Roark in popular fiction. Magazines of the period from *Popular Mechanics* to *The Saturday Evening Post* celebrated emerging personal taste. Had not World War II intervened, how different this nation might have looked and lived in the latter decades of the twentieth century.

But war did come, and one of the most remarkably rapid transformations of popular culture and mobilizations of popular will in all of history altered forever the course of the nation. The first true integrated marketing communication program may have been the massive propaganda campaign that overcame lingering doubts about American involvement in foreign affairs and enlisted every man, woman, and child in the war effort. (Ironically, communications lessons which might have been learned then were basically ignored for the next 40 years.) Every media element that existed and a few specially invented for the purpose had a single theme: defeat the Axis powers. And the objectives were not just attitudinal, but behavioral. While we were taught to hate Hitler, mock Mussolini, and despise Tojo, we were also taught the noble virtues of discipline, self-denial, and personal responsibility. Young men lined up to join the army. Children carved the shapes of enemy aircraft for spotter training and spent their precious dimes and quarters on stamps for war bonds. Older men guarded the shores and patrolled the streets. Housewives collected cooking fats, saved paper and tin and, yes, went to work in "war jobs," while grandmothers babysat by day and baked for the USO at night.

The media effort supporting all of this was pervasive and total. War dominated newspaper headlines, magazine covers, the news on radio, and newsreels in the movie theaters. Patriotic themes were woven through popular programming, comic books, and fiction. Bulletin boards in classrooms, offices, and factories; pay envelope stuffers, posters, and billboards, store windows, cereal boxes—every printed surface, moving image, or sound source went to war, just like Lucky Strike green. Never before or since has this nation of individuals been so unified in purpose, and all the changes occurred in less than half a decade.

Nowhere was this more true than in U.S. factories, converted almost entirely to war production and coordinated at the national level by businessmen pressed into government service for the war's duration.

The focus of this effort was *production:* tanks and jeeps, artillery and ammunition, fighters and bombers, and ships to carry everything to the battlefronts—no small task, with U-boat "wolf packs" sinking a million tons of Allied shipping a year.

The Manufacturing Hero

The new popular hero became the man who could get things out the factory door—the manufacturing man. The goal was more goods in less time. Design didn't matter, and quality was relative. Interchangeability was the key, and uniformity a prime virtue. People were taught to function like machines, performing repetitive functions efficiently. Factory organization structures mimicked military hierarchies.

As the war progressed, the people taking seats at the higher levels of military-style company organization charts were more and more often manufacturing men. They were the people most responsible for those "E" (for "efficiency") pennants flying next to the flag; they were the people who knew how to meet quotas. No-nonsense, roll-up-your-sleeves-and-get-it-done guys. They were the men winning the awards, making the speeches, appearing in the newsreels at the launchings and rollouts.

When the war ended, the need for their talents did not. Home came the hunters by the hundreds of thousands, energized by victory and ready to resume their interrupted lives. Meanwhile, on the home front, not only deferred maintenance but deferred dreams had created a catch-up fever. Four years of sacrifice and self-denial, four years of ration coupons, and the "little woman" was ready for some payback. Let's get married, let's have kids, let's buy a car, let's buy a house and furnish it and let's do it all *now*.

So the factories were converted back, fast, and guess what the company's most important function was? Not marketing—it hadn't been formalized yet. Not sales—the demand was already there. No, the most important function was manufacturing. Mass production. The ability to get the goods out the door. More product per minute. Quantity. And there he was, already in place—the celebrated home-front hero whose ability to produce war material made the day for the Allies and put America in a position of world dominance, the manufacturing manager, now more often than not firmly established in the executive office. The era of production-driven companies had arrived, and would stubbornly persist in some industries for 50 years or more—often long after the game had changed.

Distribution systems were set up, not surprisingly, along the military supply line model, with the orders coming from the top. Manufacturers stocked wholesalers who stocked the retailers who gratefully stocked their shelves.

"Advertising" was hyperbolic, cheerleading for the new good life—a display case in print to show Americans all the wonderful things they could own now that the war was over.

By the late 1950s, the initial surge of demand had been satisfied and the economy had begun to shift, yet production-oriented companies sought to maintain profitability by taking cost out of the manufacturing process. Efficiency experts often turned workers into machines; imagination and initiative were discouraged. Cheaper materials reduced the quality engineers had designed into products.

Mass Marketing

Mass marketing was invented to sell these standardized mass-produced products to a similarly standardized, undifferentiated mass of consumers. In 1960, the Four P's theory was articulated by a Michigan State University professor and swept through the business schools offering the new MBA degree. True to its time and culture, the formula functioned top-down and company-out; that is, it was imposed from the top and was product- rather than consumer-oriented. The manufacturer decided to make a product because it could, priced it to cover costs and to yield as much profit as possible, placed it on store shelves through the distribution chain it still dominated, and promoted it shamelessly.

The operating philosophy through all of this was caveat emptor, let the buyer beware.

The media were similarly mass-oriented, driven by advertising dollars. Radio was ubiquitous. Magazines practically gave away subscriptions, in an attempt to keep up with the new kid on the block, television, which delivered unimaginable numbers of consumers every night.

Advertisers and their agents viewed this mass audience as mindless. Advertisements, especially on television, were manipulative, formula-driven, and condescending. Jingles, slogans, and "critters" (such as Charlie the Tuna and the Jolly Green Giant) proliferated. Repetition seemed to offer fast-fast-fast results.

Actually, advertising merely reflected and reinforced the values and mores promoted by the programming. <u>Ozzie and Harriet</u>, <u>Leave It to Beaver</u>, <u>Father Knows Best</u> and countless other sitcoms illustrated the "normal" American family: mother, father, and two-point-something kids; upstanding, churchgoing people living in single-family homes in suburban neighborhoods.

Corporate leaders, who had manufacturing, engineering, or financial functions, were uncomfortable with a "soft science" like advertising. While they allowed themselves to be persuaded that it was necessary, most would agree with the sentiment often ascribed to Philadelphia merchant John Wanamaker: "I know that 50 percent of my advertising dollars are wasted; trouble is, I don't know which 50 percent." But while the lack of hard measurements bothered business leaders in the abstract, the reality was that lots of advertising correlated with the movement of lots of goods. No one knew why, but it appeared to work. And the country was riding the crest of a huge wave of economic expansion that swept the world through the 1960s. If we were a little imprecise in our methods, so what? Maybe it takes a little faith to work an economic miracle.

To be sure, there were voices warning that no tree grows to the sky, that old habits would not serve in new times, warning against misread history and false confidence.

As early as 1960, Harvard's Ted Levitt wrote in *Marketing Myopia*, "There's no such thing as a growth industry. There are only consumer needs, which might shift at any time." But millions watched Dustin Hoffman's drunken uncle whisper in the ear of the graduate, "Plastics, my boy. Plastics." A sure thing, they nodded.

Levitt spoke further, challenging other sacred truths. Henry Ford is celebrated for the wrong thing, he said. Yes, he applied Samuel Colt's mass production techniques to the manufacturing of automobiles, but that was just implementation. His true genius was in seeing the need for cheap motorized transportation in the first place, for recognizing an enormous potential market, an unsatisfied popular craving. Latter-day auto company managers, Levitt argued, spend too much time on processes and other aspects of running the business and not enough time tracking customer needs and wants, the only reason for the business to exist at all. But 60 percent of all the world's cars, trucks, and buses at that time were made in Detroit. What did that pointy-head from Harvard know?

Demassification

In 1970, in *Future Shock*, Alvin Toffler coined the word "demassification" and went on to predict much of the flying-apart of the social structure that the nation would experience in the next decade. But even if he were right, people argued, what could be done with such knowledge? Better not to think about it! Eyes glazed over. As Saul Bellow had the title character in *Augie March* say, "People create a world they can live in, and what they can't use, they often can't see."

In the early '70s, creative leaders in General Electric's huge advertising and sales promotion operation developed a theory called FOCUS which postulated that "All good advertising begins with a fundamental understanding of the receiver." "Receiver" was shorthand for a prototypical individual whose behavior the advertising was intended to influence. But that's not how advertising was done, at GE or anywhere else. Instead, the client typically called up the advertising agency account exec and said, "Do me an ad on the new (insert name of product)." The account exec went to the client's factory or office, sometimes with the copywriter, and collected information about the product. If the product was a technical one, they were admitted to the Presence of Engineering, and told more about the product's wondrous properties.

Back at the shop, the agency rendered an ad about the product, one that was at least descriptive and, ideally, clever. The ad went back through an approval process innocent of reference to its intended target. "That's why," said prominent researcher Dr. George Gallup in 1970, "advertising has improved so little in the quarter century following the second World War—it focuses entirely on the product and not at all on the prospect."

But who cared? Business was good and growth seemed endless. Gathering information about the receiver was not anyone's priority, and what little data existed was hard to analyze and manipulate. Research reports just gathered dust on shelves or vanished into desk drawers.

In 1972, Jack Trout and Al Ries articulated the "positioning theory," which attacked the fact that most marketing plans were conceived as though products existed in isolation. Critics sneered that the authors were just trying to develop a gimmick. "We've always positioned our products," the critics said, thereby demonstrating the authors' point perfectly. "Advertisers and agencies don't position product," Trout and Ries said, "consumers do." Companies need to determine what position their products already occupy in the customer's mind relative to other products; only then can they act to reinforce or change that position. What's in the consumer's mind is far more important than what comes out of the marketing war room. But few understood the subtlety; fewer still thought that it mattered.

Another voice began to be heard on other subjects early in the 1970s. A decade before he published *Megatrends*, John Naisbitt warned in his *Trend Reports* that consumer attitudes on social issues such as the environment would before long affect their purchasing behavior. Not many executives had the patience to listen to ideas so seemingly far-removed from their bottom-line concerns, much less the imagination to plan early to put their companies in a position to profit in case Naisbitt proved to be right.

Then again, why should they? The king was in his counting house and all was right with the world. Sure, the social aberrations of the 1960s had raised some uncomfortable questions, and the OPEC business had led to some dislocation, but on the whole the country was still on track.

Almost without warning, however—at least without warning that most thought to heed—world economies passed through one of Drucker's "great divides." Growth rates from 1973 through 1987 almost without exception averaged half the 1950–1973 rates.

Some thought (or hoped) that this, too, was temporary. Doggedly, they persisted in old habits, and too often watched as the world went by.

Other people apparently decided that *everything* was temporary and behaved as though there were no tomorrow, or at least there was nothing they could count on beyond the current fiscal quarter. The future, they said, was 90 days out. Make the numbers and move on. The fast track awaited.

The result was an explosion of social and economic experimentation—not to say irresponsibility—that in retrospect looks like the night sky on the Fourth of July.

Empowerment

As the '90s dawned, new realities were visible which are reshaping the world as we know it and the way existing companies must behave to profit in it.

Globally, the military-style hierarchies were (and are) crumbling. Top-down management worked only as long as the parties in power controlled the communications channels. "Channels of command" was an apt phrase in its time, but its time was past. The new phrase is "empowerment."

Empowerment means that people not only choose what they wish to listen to, but also that they talk back and have the means to make themselves heard. Wise rulers, those who keep their heads, hear and obey, as do wise business managers, those who keep their jobs and their companies.

In the United States, the social and economic landscape on either side of the "great divide" is as profoundly different as the Rockies are different from the Plains.

The family unit has been redefined. In 1960, 60 percent of families included three or more members; 20 percent included five or more. By 1990, the Leave it to Beaver family of mother, father, and two kids comprised only 7 percent of households. Sixty percent had two or fewer members, and more than half of all new households formed were singles. The implications for marketing: less pressure to conform to "family" values; more lifestyle options considered; *basic* household needs (e.g. furnishings and kitchen appliances) multiplied. Also, families with fewer children spend more on each child, a phenomenon magnified by guilt in single-parent homes and in homes where both parents work.

Where once only adverturesome spirits left the old hometown, now both young and old are more likely to move away from their families. This new mobility weakens the "tribal" influence and encourages individual thinking; as options multiply, so do basic household needs.

Educational levels are higher, despite public concern over issues such as declining SAT scores. In 1960, fewer than 15 percent of high school graduates attended college. By 1990, that number had climbed to 54 percent. Companies hired MBAs to sell cardboard boxes, and they were talking to MBAs on the other side of the desk. Implications for marketers: better educated people are harder to fool. They can accept—even demand—more sophisticated information, and they will read the fine print.

Old Dad is no longer the only breadwinner; 54 percent of mothers with children under 17 are in the workforce, and they're not tourists—42 percent believe themselves to be in a career, not just a job. This contributes to historically high employment levels in this country, not counting the huge number of off-the-book jobs that contribute to a burgeoning underground economy. Implications for marketers: recessions are cushioned by great if latent buying power; the need for service is multiplied with Mom no longer home to do everything; and time becomes the new currency. A sidebar: Mom outside the home is exposed to new ideas, further threatening assumptions about traditional family values.

The population is older. During the decade of the '90s, a baby-boomer will turn 50 every nine seconds! Contrary to conventional wisdom, this is an accelerant to change. One survey reported that senior citizens identified their number one pleasure as "Trying new things." No wonder. They are free of responsibility, the kids are gone, and the mortgages are paid off. They have lots of disposable income. Senior citizens in the '60s had thrived through the post-World War II expansion, but they remembered the Depression: they were savers. Seniors today have the highest concentration of wealth of any population segment and the lowest percent at the poverty level. They're also healthier than older people used to be, thanks to better diets and advances in medicine. And they read: the number one magazine in circulation is *Modern Maturity*, published by the Association for the Advancement of Retired People (AARP).

Media options are exploding. In 1960, network television delivered over 90 percent of U.S. households. By 1990, the number was under two-thirds and declining. (By 1991, network viewing was under 50 percent in prime time on Saturday night!) Meanwhile, cable became ubiquitous, and to complicate the video picture, more than two billion video cassettes were purchased in 1990 alone. Print was just as fragmented; Standard Rate and Data Service (SRDS) identified 11,400 magazines in circulation that year.

Future Trends

The collapse of the mass media—not only the once-pervasive broadcasting networks, but magazines of the 1950s such as *Life*, *Look*, and *The Saturday Evening Post*—shook to the foundations the whole system upon which marketing and advertising were based. The mass media provided advertisers with access to the mass market at a low unit cost, the perfect mirror for the then-prevailing mass production mentality. But the mass media also *taught* mass culture. Programs such as Leave It to Beaver, Ozzie and Harriet, and Father Knows Best reinforced shared values, complemented by Norman Rockwell covers and pictures in print of prototypical American families at work, at home, and at play.

Marketing functioned so efficiently in 1960, just like the modern American factory. But by 1990, nearly everything seemed to have turned upside down. The faces in the crowd loomed larger than the crowd itself.

As much as the mass media and particularly network TV were enablers and abetters of the mass marketing mentality, so have computers—and particularly universal access to computers —been both the cause of the age of the individual and marketing's key to coping with it.

The ability to collect, store, access, and manipulate data, to turn data into information and apply it, in the laboratory, on the manufacturing floor, in the marketing department, and yes, in the home, changed everything.

Computers accelerated data analysis and homogenized design. Competitors could break your formula before you had a product out of testing. This destroyed the old manufacturing-driven idea that one had years to reap profits from new products by milking market share while cutting costs. Computers devalued technological superiority and revalued marketing. Even if products became similar, strategies could be different.

But can they? Computers gave everybody instant access to information. For a price—and a low price, at that—marketers monitor every element of a competitor's strategy through any of a half-dozen reporting services and track the results through scanner data. There are no secrets.

Computers gave capital value to information and shifted power away from the manufacturer.

But computers giveth even as they taketh away. Even if the strategies are the same, a marketer can use the power of computers to gain a competitive advantage by developing superior insight into the mind of the customer. Suddenly the FOCUS philosophy—"All good advertising begins with a fundamental understanding of the receiver"—is implementable. Information about the receiver is available and accessible as never before.

The consumer, freed from the lockstep of uniform opinion, develops his or her own tastes and finds new power as manufacturers scurry to respond.

Economies of scale no longer guarantee profitability. Giant centralized manufacturing facilities give way to customized, quick-change plants, close to differentiated markets. Niche marketing replaces mass marketing. Suddenly, cost reduction can be costly if it results in reduced customer satisfaction. Quality is no longer determined by manufacturing standards, but rather by customer perceptions of price/value. And elements of manufacturing discretion such as ethical sourcing, workplace health and safety, and environmental responsibility become part of the product. Decisions must be made on other than cost-based economics.

Distribution is no longer a marketer's decision. The consumer decides how, where, and when he or she wishes to buy, and the marketer had better be there.

> Your product is only available at Nordstrom, which is only open from 10:00 to 5:00? I'll sit in bed with my curlers on at two o'clock in the morning and buy your competitor's product out of a catalog, using my phone and a credit card.

> Your product is only found on grocery shelves in standard sizes? I'll buy your competitor's product in a ten-gallon drum at a membership discount store.

Retailers, pressed by their customers and empowered by suddenly precious information about those customers which they may uniquely possess, talk back to manufacturers, make demands, and take control.

What happened to the orderly world of the Four P's? They turned into Lauterborn's Four C's.

The new catechism said:

> Forget Product. Study Consumer wants and needs. You can no longer sell whatever you can make. You can only sell what someone specifically wants to buy.

The feeding frenzy was over; the fish were out of school. Now marketers had to learn to lure them one by one, with something each customer particularly wanted.

> Forget Price. Understand the consumer's Cost to satisfy that want or need.

Marketers needed to understand that to many "New Age" consumers, price is almost irrelevant; dollars are only one part of the cost. What someone selling hamburgers might be selling against is not just another burger for a few cents more or less. It's the cost of time to drive somewhere, the cost of conscience to eat meat at all, and the cost of guilt for not treating the kids. Value is no longer the biggest burger for the cheapest price, it's a complex equation with as many different correct solutions as there are subsets of customers.

> Forget Place. Think Convenience to buy.

People don't have to go anyplace anymore, in this era of catalogs, credit cards, and 800 numbers. Marketers need to learn to think beyond those nice, neat, controlled distribution channels they set up over the years. They need to learn how each subsegment of the market prefers to buy, and then how to be there.

> Finally, forget Promotion. The word in the '90s is Communication.

The motto of the age of the manufacturer—*caveat emptor*, let the buyer beware—is replaced by *cave emptorum*, beware of the buyer.

Integration

Enter a new age of advertising: respectful, not patronizing; dialogue-seeking, not monologuic; responsive, not formula-driven. It speaks to the highest point of common interest, not the lowest common denominator. (Contrast Charlie the Tuna with messages about dolphin-safe fishing practices; kitchen dramas with green packaging.) And advertising often isn't "advertising" at all, to the extent that advertising means commercials on radio and television and print ads in magazines and newspapers.

Moreover, marketers no longer view advertising as a necessary evil, a little understood or controllable element of cost. More and more, advertising is perceived as an investment, and as such is held accountable for specific results.

Advertisers, their agencies, and the media modify their relationships to serve new roles, and integrated marketing communication (IMC) emerges, albeit tentatively.

For IMC to really take hold, old assumptions must exit, assumptions about the role of advertising and sales promotion, about the organization of advertising and public relations departments, about agencies and what they do, about the media, and most of all, about accountability.

Smart marketers and their agents everywhere are in the process of "sloughing off the old, the dying, the obsolete," in Peter Drucker's words.

> Innovating organizations spend neither time nor resources defending yesterday. Systematic abandonment of yesterday alone can free the resources —and especially the scarcest resource of them all, capable people—for work on the new.

The "new" of integrated marketing communications will require much tearing down.

Capable people in client organizations are trapped in functional boxes, constrained and trained not to solve business problems but to "do advertising" or "do public relations" or "do direct marketing."

Advertising agencies see their role as producing media advertising. Most added below-the-line services only to capture client dollars they perceived as slipping from their grasp. Sales promotion, direct marketing, public relations, and other units may be sailing under the same flag, but it's a flag of convenience. These service areas are still separate and by no means equal.

Most agencies see their own competitive advantage as deriving from one of two organizing principles: superior client service or superior creative.

Fewer than a handful of advertising agencies have even begun to recognize that the most precious thing they have to sell today is a fundamental understanding of the receiver and what motivates that receiver. Jay Chiat brought the account planning function over from Britain. When dark horse Chiat/Day won the $180 million Nissan account, the client said, "All the other agencies talked to us about the car business; Chiat/Day impressed us with their understanding of the car *buyer*." Los Angeles Saatchi & Saatchi subsidiary Team One has taken the concept a step further. The agency repositioned itself to specialize in selling to upscale consumers. The product doesn't matter—high-end cars, furs, even real estate. Radical thinking, and right.

This receiver-focus rather than product-focus frees "capable people" everywhere in the agency to contribute creatively. In fact, DDB Needham CEO Keith Reinhard calls the media department "the other creative department," and says that a campaign is as likely to be constructed around a media concept as a creative concept, or to be led by a media event supported by public relations, direct marketing and, oh yes, advertising.

Whatever works. But this open-mindedness is still exceptional. As a rule, agencies talk about "orchestration" and integration, but when they sit down to play, the first line is, "So what should the ads say?"

One change-driver may be altered compensation systems. "I hear what you say but I see how you pay," agencies may respond to clients who ask for fresh thinking and alternative media suggestions, but who cling to prehistoric commission systems which reward business-as-usual thinking.

Inexorably, however, compensation systems are beginning to reflect the dreaded "A-word," accountability. Client company senior managements are asking tough return-on-investment questions, which in turn forces advertisers and agencies to think through the whole process of making a sale, and to try to control any element that could have an impact on profitability. More than any other factor, the pressure for accountability will open the system and cause the changes that will make thinking in terms of integrated marketing communication not only possible, but inevitable.

Major media mergers such as the creation of Time-Warner and its subsequent acquisition of Whittle are accelerating the process. Time-Warner is packaging multiple media to deliver not just rating points but measured results in the marketplace. Indeed, ex-chairman Dick Munro actually defined Time-Warner as "a direct marketing company." Harvard's Ted Levitt, author of the seminal marketing treatise *Marketing Myopia*, would surely agree. Time didn't fight windmills to defend its magazine business. It recognized that it is really in the business of satisfying customer needs—the needs of its advertising customers to sell products— and moved aggressively to assemble a more potent resource.

The retraining requirements implied in advertising/marketing changes for advertisers, agencies, and the media alike are daunting. David Ogilvy notes that integrated marketing communication calls for "a completely new breed of account executives, who are trained in all the disciplines." Complicating the problem, he warns, is the fact that, "Too many people who are paid to write advertising are not interested in selling. They talk about creativity all the time. In the new world," he says, "we sell or else."

Ogilvy's and several other companies are already involved in the retraining task, and this also will accelerate the trend. As philosopher Alfred North Whitehead observed, "That which is taught, is considered possible."

2

How Marketing Communications Works:
Or at Least, How We Think It Works

▼

Most of us who work in the marketing communications business today grew up during the years mass communication developed in the United States and around the world. Over the past 40 years or so, we have seen advertising, sales promotion, direct marketing, public relations, and all the other forms of marketing communications become very complex and sophisticated industries. But just as we were watching the field of marketing communications mature, we started to see it change. Perhaps that is what has been so surprising—the incredibly fast change from mass marketing to one-on-one marketing, from mass communication to individual communication, from what we knew and were comfortable with to things that seem to challenge the very nature of our businesses and our lives. In an incredibly short period of time, we have seen the rise and now seeming decline of mass media; the move from local media to global electronic communications systems; the shift from planned, scheduled media events to instantaneous communication between persons and organizations; the change from time- and place-bound communications systems to time-shifting by consumers to fit their needs and their schedules. And these are just a few of the changes the past decade brought. While many of these changes are the result of technological innovation, many other human development factors have caused this communication revolution, too. Whatever the cause and result, all have contributed to the increasing need for a new and radically different view of marketing communications that takes into account changes that likely will occur in the next few years and into the new century. In our view, all have and will continue to create the demand for integrated marketing communications.

In this chapter, we look first at some of the changes that have occurred in communications and communications technology. Then we look at the human factors involved in marketing communications. We relate these changes and our better understanding of how marketing communications works to the demand for integrated marketing communications programs that will replace the traditional functional and media-specific approaches on which many marketing organizations still rely. We conclude with some of the critical communications issues that make integrated marketing communications important to all types of marketing organizations.

How Communications Changed

Few consumers today can recall the period prior to the existence of mass media systems in the United States. Network radio and television, national magazines, and large metropolitan daily newspapers seem to have always been with us. These systems not only tied the country together, but there is strong evidence that to a great extent they helped create our social and political culture. Since everyone could, and often did, see and perhaps hear the same messages at the same time from the 1950s to the 1970s, we created an almost homogeneous mass media and mass marketing culture. Marketing organizations created broadly demanded products for these mass markets. Retail distribution systems developed to sell to and through these markets. And marketing communications professionals developed plans, programs, and systems to communicate to these mass markets.

The marketing systems created in the United States worked like well-oiled machines through the mid-1980s. Then technology collided with society and human wants and needs. Suddenly consumers, who now had more information than ever before, began to demand specialized products, distribution systems, and communication. What once had been a mass market splintered into hundreds if not thousands of separate, individual markets driven by lifestyle, ethnic background, income, geography, education, gender, and all the other things that make one person different from another.

While scores of reasons have been given for this "demassification" of the American marketplace, we focus on just four here because they are so directly related to how both marketers and consumers use marketing communications on an almost daily basis.

From Verbal to Visual

If you are over the age of 40, there's a good chance you were raised as a verbal communicator. You were trained throughout your school years in spelling, grammar, how to parse sentences, how not to dangle participles, and so on. The emphasis was on writing and reading skills. Therefore, you are, like your parents before you, a member of a verbal generation.

If you're under 40, chances are you're a member of the visual generation. This generation was raised on television, movies, speeches, MTV, and the spoken word. The educational emphasis, although we don't like to acknowledge it, was on sounds, symbols, signs, pictures, and icons with which you learned to communicate with others and through which others learned to communicate with you.

The difference between how these two generations communicate is tremendous. An example will help explain further.

Learning to operate a computer is an increasingly easy task. Both hardware and software have become more user friendly. If we look back a few years, we can begin to see a difference in how each of us learned to use a computer. The verbal generation was taught to use a computer through a step-by-step system. The process was logical, orderly, and consistent. Think about how you learned to operate a computer. You started with Lesson One and progressed to Lesson Two and then Three and so on. It was a slow, sometimes tedious process, but eventually you learned and you likely learned well because that is the way you learned everything else.

Look at how teenagers learn how to use a computer today. They flip on the machine. Jam in a disk. Beat on the keys to see what works and what doesn't. They ask a few friends. Beat on the keys a bit more. Finally, they learn what works and what doesn't, what happens when one does some things and what doesn't happen when one does other things. In essence, today's youngsters learn to use computers by doing, by trial-and-error, and by the use of icons, symbols, signs, and yes, even with a mouse. And they seem to learn faster and better and perhaps more effectively than the generations before them. Think what the impact of this move from verbal to visual communication is having and will continue to have on computer instructional manuals, help sheets, and even programs and software. This same sort of change from verbal to visual is occurring throughout society—a dramatic change in how we communicate.

The shift from a verbal to a visual society will continue to be a major factor in why integrated marketing communications will be so necessary for marketing organizations in the years to come.

Functional Illiteracy

With the move from a verbal to a visual society has come a major social problem, *functional* illiteracy. Traditionally, illiteracy has been defined as an inability to read or to comprehend written materials. Our problem today, however, is the growing percentage of the population that is functionally illiterate, able to read some words but unable to comprehend simple sentences, phrases, or instructions. Though the functionally illiterate person technically is able to read, to understand words, he or she lacks the ability to put these words into meaningful structures that will allow functioning in an increasingly complex world.

Some people argue that the shift from a verbal to a visual society has increased the number of functional illiterates in the population. They say we have reduced the need to read by increasing the use of graphics and icons. The visualization of material allows people to survive and even to perform in a functionally illiterate state. For example, one need only look at the cash register at a fast food restaurant to see how visualization has removed the need for reading or literacy. The cash register is coded with symbols, not words; the machine calculates the change to be rendered; the products are color coded with wrappers; and so on. So while functional illiteracy is a major problem in the workforce, it is as large a problem for the marketer, too.

As functional illiteracy grows in the United States, marketers will increasingly need to use symbols, icons, pictures, sounds, and other forms of communication to send messages to customers and prospects. As they do, the need to integrate these various forms of communication will become more and more important. As the marketer relies increasingly on communication techniques that reach the literate, functionally illiterate, and even illiterate to deliver a sales messages, the demand for integrated marketing communications will become increasingly important.

Media Fragmentation

Technology has played a tremendous role in creating a demand for integrated marketing communications. At one time the advertiser, by purchasing commercials on the three television networks, could, during an average week, reach up to 90 percent of the U.S. population. Today that number has fallen to 60 percent or less and will likely continue to decline. The mass media no longer deliver masses (or at least attractive masses) for many marketing organizations.

Technology has allowed media organizations to begin identifying, segmenting, selecting, and attracting smaller, more attentive and focused audiences for their audio, video, and print vehicles. There is even talk of one-on-one marketing through various forms of marketing communications. While one-on-one marketing communications is technically feasible today, the cost is still prohibitive. However, it may not be so in the future.

Logically, it would seem, media fragmentation works against the concept of integrated marketing communications. If we could selectively reach individuals with media messages, then there would be no need to integrate. Each message would stand on its own. With more selective media, there would be no real reason to integrate. The problem is, however, that while the individual audience for each of the media has become smaller, there are more and more media to which the customer or prospect is exposed. Thus, the marketer's prospect may take one message from a television show, another from radio, and still another from the newspaper. In addition, as we shall see shortly when we discuss how communication works in today's marketplace, the consumer today tends to lump all persuasive messages into something they call "advertising." Thus, consumers don't differentiate among advertising messages in a medium such as television or a magazine or an outdoor display. Consumers don't even differentiate among the various functional approaches used by marketers, such as advertising, sales promotion, direct mail, or even public relations and advertorials. Messages are all just part of "advertising" or in some cases "product information" and they are seemingly all lumped together in the minds of the customers or prospects. So, no matter from what medium the information or message came, the information is seen as just a media message. And, no matter what the message said, it stands for the brand, the company, or the marketing organization. We'll discuss the chunking or categorization system that customers and prospects use to gather, store, and use information in the next section.

The system of information storage used by consumers makes integrated marketing communications such a critical issue today and tomorrow. As we start to understand more about how people process information and about the specifics of communication, we will understand why integrated marketing communications is so important. We will say more on that in the next section.

Growth of the Value and Importance of Perceptions versus Facts

One of the major issues marketers face is the increasing reliance of consumers and prospects on perceptions rather than facts when they make purchasing decisions. Simply put, there is increasing evidence that customers and prospects are basing most of their purchasing decisions on what they perceive to be important or true or what they think is right or correct rather than on solid, rational, economically derived information.

Part of this shift in how consumers make purchasing decisions is a result of the promotional activities of marketers themselves during the past few years. As marketers have shifted more and more of their marketing communication funds to price promotion such as discounts, rebates, and coupons, they seem to have convinced consumers that many of the products on the shelf are pretty much the same. The product selection is at parity and the only differentiating feature among products is price. Thus when price is the deciding factor, price becomes uppermost in the decision process and product features become less and less important. In effect, whatever information a person needs to make a purchasing decision from among these perceived parity products can be gathered at the store shelf.

But it is not just the belief that product parity exists that makes people believe product information isn't very important. What we seem to find in case after case is that people have less and less product information in a marketplace that is ever richer in product data. In other words, we now live in an age of "sound bite decision making." As we have increased the flow and volume of data, consumers have been forced to find ways to cope with the cacophony of information around them. What they apparently have decided to do is simply to skim the surface, gather bits and pieces, weave the bits and pieces into some sort of knowledge or decision fabric, and be on their way. In other words, people today take in and process enough information to allow them to understand or muddle through on most subjects. They limit their information to the least they need to know. Thus, while consumers know a little bit about many things, they don't know very much about anything. They know just enough to get by.

This increasing consumer reliance on perceptions or the gathering of small bits of information about a product or service will be a growing challenge to marketers. As consumers decide they have enough product information on which to make a purchase decision, they naturally will tend to ignore more information or data that conflict with what they already know. To the consumer, perception is truth. A perception may not be correct but it is what they know, and what they know is all they need to know.

This new "sound bite" approach to gathering marketing information demands that a marketer's statements about products or services must be clear, consistent, and comprehensible. In the fast-paced, information-overloaded marketplace of the 1990s, integrated marketing communications on behalf of a product or service will be vital. If perceptions are reality to consumers, then the perceptions which the marketer delivers must be consistent through all forms of communication or the consumer will simply ignore them.

What we have described above are just a few of the communications-related issues that will increase the demand for integrated marketing communications today and into the future. These factors are closely related to what we have learned about how consumers select, take in, process, store, and recall information from the marketplace. Once we understand that process, we can begin to understand how critical integrated marketing communications is and will be to all types of marketing organizations.

Understanding Information Processing

As suggested in the previous section, the real reason integrated marketing communications programs are needed is the result of what we have learned and what we are still learning about how humans select, take in, process, and store information and experiences and then how they use this information in making future purchasing decisions. This process has a number of names but for simplicity we will call it information processing.

There are two major factors in the broad process of information processing. The first is the concept of perception; how we select, process, and store information in memory. The second is directly related and has to do with how we access, add to, and use the information that we have previously stored. While the two are almost indistinguishable in use, we will separate them for purposes of explaining the process.

Perception, or What We Put into Our Heads

To understand communication and why integrated marketing communications is such a critical issue in today's marketplace, we must first understand how people select from the sights, sounds, sensations, and experiences constantly bombarding them from their environment. We must also understand how what is selected is stored, and then how it is categorized and retrieved from the mind. This process is generally called perception. It is illustrated in Exhibit 2-1.

The process of perception is an active system. Every waking second we are actively selecting from all the sights, sounds, sensations, activities, and impressions that surround us. From the myriad of choices, we pick those things we either want to or must process and consider those that, for some reason, get our attention. (We'll talk more about attention later.)

Because the number of sensations in our environment is so much greater than our ability to process them, we select only those things that we perceive to be important and we ignore those that aren't. Thus, we limit our span of perception.

To help us handle all these bits and pieces of data we use a system called transformation and categorization. This helps us to simplify and classify items and aids in the selection and storage process. In other words, we transform the sights, sounds, and

▼   **Exhibit 2-1**

Model of the Perceptual Process

Source: Dennis W. Organ and Thomas S. Bateman, *Organizational Behavior*, 4th ed. (Homewood, III.: Irwin, 1991), 130.

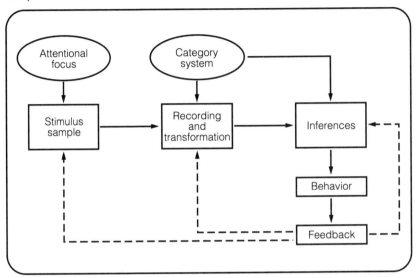

sensations around us and put them into a sort of sensible form we call a concept. These concepts can then be stored in our memory. Thus, a very complex human product like the jet airplane may be simplified into one or only a few concepts for mental storage. Concepts may have much detail attached or related to them. For ease of storage and retrieval, we compact the bits and pieces of information into a singular concept that can be stored in the mind.

From these concepts, we then create categories. The categories enable us to further classify and store information. For example, the category of travel may contain multiple concepts such as a vehicle, lodging, meals, sights, other people's cultures, and so on. Through the transformation and categorization process, we are able to store relatively large amounts of data and information in our minds with only a few concepts and categories. The categorization scheme allows us to function in our very complex environment.

Based on the concepts we have stored and the categories we have created, we are able to make assumptions and inferences about things when we have a new experience or when we consider stored concepts and categories. For example, when confronted with the category of "school," we call up several concepts about "schools" that we have stored away. We may have categorized schools into kindergartens, primary, secondary, or high schools, or colleges and universities. Therefore, when we consider the category of schools and the more specific concept of "a primary school," we may assume the school is attended by younger people, that it is located in a neighborhood, that there are teachers present, and so on. Further, we can infer from the concept of "primary school" that the emphasis in the classroom is probably on reading, writing, and arithmetic and not on physics, calculus, or advanced computer programming. Thus the storage of the simplified categories and concepts allows us to keep a vast amount of information in a limited amount of storage.

The process of perception is basic in understanding the need for integrated marketing communications in the 1990s. The transformation and categorization process that people use to select, take in, process and store information is very limited, given the sensations and stimuli that surround us. Information processing is taking place at all times. Because we have such a limited ability to process and store information, we can quickly see why, if the sales message from a marketer is to be selected and processed, it must

1   consist of sights, sounds, and experiences that can be transformed easily into concepts and then be categorized in the mind,

2   be clearly identifiable and categorizable, and

3   fit into the categories that people have already created.

Marketing communications messages that are not recognizable, are not related to each other, conflict with what has already been stored, or are simply unrelated or unimportant to the person simply will not be processed. As the world become more complex and as people spend more time selecting information that will help them with the important task of living, there will be less time and space for information, data, or concepts about the marketer's product or service. The marketer must therefore provide reasons for the person to process his or her information.

With this understanding of perception, we can now use perception to explain how we believe people deal with marketing communications messages in today's marketplace.

How Communications Works through the Processing System

Marketing communications messages—such things as advertising, sales promotion, direct marketing, public relations, special events, or trade shows—all seek to do one thing: to place bits of information in the customer's or prospect's mind that hopefully will influence future purchase decisions. Our knowledge of information processing supports the idea that previous good experiences or favorable information that the consumer has stored in his or her mind will influence the purchase of a specific product or service when a decision is being made. To understand this communication-influence-purchase process, we must understand how persuasive messages are delivered, processed, and stored by customers and prospects.

The most basic model of communication is based on a stimulus-response system. It is illustrated in Exhibit 2-2 below.

We call this the interpersonal communication model because it illustrates how face-to-face communication works. There

▼ *Exhibit 2-2*

Interpersonal Model

Source: Adapted from Wilbur Schramm and Donald Roberts, eds., *The Process and Effects of Mass Communication* (Urbana, Ill.: University of Illinois Press, 1971).

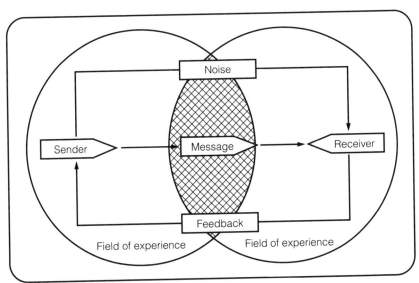

is a sender, a message, and a receiver. There is also a feedback loop. The feedback tells the sender whether or not the receiver has received the message. At the top of the model there is a process called "noise." This acknowledges that outside interference may prevent the receiver from receiving the message. Noise may be interruptions in the sender-message-receiver channel or a distraction when the message was being delivered. It is also possible that the message becomes garbled in some way and cannot be processed by the receiver.

The two large circles represent the fields of experience of the sender and the receiver. These are the perceptions in the form of concepts and categories that the sender and receiver have stored away and to which they have access. Either the sender must understand what the receiver has stored or the receiver must have some background in the area of the message. Otherwise there will likely be no communication.

These fields of experience of the sender and receiver are critically important to the process of communication. The model gives us the first clue of why integrated marketing communications is so critical in today's overcommunicated world. For communication to occur, the message sender must understand the receiver's fields of experience or the receiver must have some background in the marketer's message area.

We can also see from this interpersonal model that present-day mass media communication flows in only one direction, from the sender or marketer to the receiver or consumer. This process is what creates so much waste and ineffectiveness in today's marketing communications programs.

Our concept of integrated marketing communications is based on the need for a continual exchange of information and experiences between the marketer and the customer. The marketer seeks and stores information on each individual customer in a database. The customer, through transactions, surveys, and other methods is encouraged to communicate back to the marketer. Thus the fields of experience of both become greater and more useful to both parties. This relationship approach is central to our philosophy of integrated marketing communications.

Using the interpersonal communication model and the concept of the fields of experience, we can start to understand how marketing communications works in today's marketplace.

How Marketing Communications Works

Exhibit 2-3 illustrates a simplified model of how today's marketing communications flows between the marketer and the consumer.

▼ *Exhibit 2-3*

How Marketing Communications Works

Source: Don E. Schultz and Stanley I. Tannenbaum, *Essentials of Advertising Strategy*, 2nd ed. (Lincolnwood, Ill.: NTC Business Books, 1989), 32.

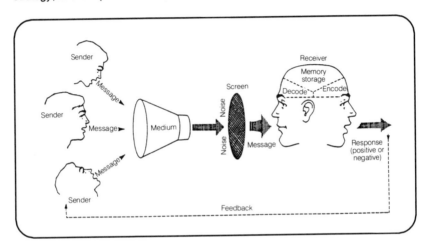

In the marketplace, there are numerous marketers trying to deliver their sales messages to customers or prospects. As the communications delivery systems have grown and the number of marketers has increased there is almost a babble in the marketplace. As we discussed earlier, consumers have limited information processing capabilities. So as the number of message senders increases and the messages they attempt to send multiplies, the confusion in the marketplace grows.

The marketers are also sending their sales messages through a myriad of media. In our illustration we showed only one. In truth, however, there are hundreds of media vehicles available to marketing organizations. As the number of media increase, the noise in the channel grows. Thus greater numbers of the marketer's messages don't get through or are lost in the system. Unfortunately, in today's marketplace our methods of measuring this loss are quite primitive, but we do know there is increasing waste in the marketing communications budget.

From the available messages, the consumer actively selects those to be processed. The selection system is impacted by the media systems to which the consumer is exposed. If there is no media exposure, there can be no communication. So another important consideration in our concept of integrated marketing communications is the coordination of media messages.

From the thousands of marketing communications messages to which the consumer is exposed each day, the consumer chooses a relatively small number to process. When we say thousands of sales messages per day we are not exaggerating. We include as media messages all the sights, sounds, stimuli, and bits of information that contain the name, icon, symbol, or thought of the advertiser. This expanded view of a sales message is critical to our view of integrated marketing communications.

As explained earlier, the consumer actively selects the messages to be processed. The first step in this process is that of decoding the parts of the marketer's message. To communicate, we have developed a complex system of codes that carry certain meanings. For instance, words are codes, as are sounds and smells. The method in which the marketer puts these codes together is intended to produce a meaning or to represent a group of concepts or a category in the consumer's mind. Thus when a consumer sees an advertisement illustrated with a happy dog, tail wagging, eagerly eating a bowl of dog food, the message the consumer likely takes away is that the dog in the picture likes the dog food and that the consumer's dog would probably like it also.

Problems occur when the marketer uses codes or concepts with which the receiver is not familiar. The most obvious example is a foreign language. If this paragraph were written in Chinese or Korean characters, most likely a number of American readers would not be able to understand the code. Another example might be a lack of understanding by you as a reader if a popular novel were filled with mathematical equations or scientific notation. As we can see, a critical ingredient in any form of marketing communications is the use of codes that have the same meaning to both the marketer and the consumer.

Once the consumer decodes the message, he or she has two choices. One is an immediate response to the message. In this case, little or no processing or memory storage is required. An example of this is when the consumer is shopping in a store.

Toothpaste is on the shopping list. When the customer nears the toothpaste aisle, she sees a display with a special sign for Acme Toothpaste, one of her favorite brands. The sign says the price is reduced. The customer quickly matches the reduced price on the sign with the stored price information on Acme Toothpaste in her mind. She finds that the price is, indeed, a bargain and picks up the product for purchase. Thus, the marketer of Acme Toothpaste has received an immediate response to the marketing communications message in the form of a sale. As marketers, we categorize these forms of direct response to our marketing communications programs as sales promotion, direct marketing, or merchandising.

For many other types of marketing communications messages, the consumer's response is not so direct. Often, the customer or prospect is not in the market for the promoted product. While the marketing communications message may be received and processed, it will not result in immediate action and there may not be any communication feedback. Instead, the consumer may store the message for later use by attaching it to the concept or category in which the product is kept in the mind. Thus while the marketer has no direct measure that his or her marketing communication message had any impact, the message may well have been added to the concept of the brand, the product form, or the category for later use.

Since few consumers are in the market for a given product or service at any one time, many of today's marketing communications messages are being stored in the consumer's mind. Therefore it is important for the marketer to know how this mental storage system is organized and how consumers add to, change, or retrieve this marketing communications information.

Communication of a marketing sales message is said to occur when the consumer accepts, transforms, and categorizes the message. The storage and retrieval system works on the basis of matching incoming information with what is already stored in memory. If the information matches or enhances what is already there, then the new information will likely be added to the existing concepts and categories. If it doesn't, the consumer has to make a choice, either the new information can replace what is already there or the new information can be rejected. In this case, the consumer would continue to use existing concepts and categories. We call this the "judgment system" in that consumers match or

▼   **Exhibit 2-4**
Judgment Model

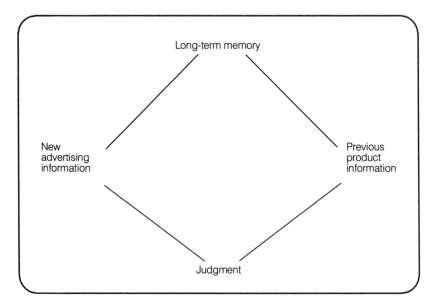

test new information against what they already have and then make a judgment to add to, adapt, or reject. The process is illustrated in Exhibit 2-4.

If the new information is added to the customer's store of knowledge about the brand or product or if it is attached in some way through adjustment of previous concepts or categories, we say we have "communicated." When consumers reject the information or do not add or attach it to what they already have, we say we have failed to communicate. In many cases, this failure to communicate is the result of the marketer being unable to match his or her messages or fields of experience with those of the prospect or customer.

To understand how critical this judgment is to the success of the marketing communications program, we must understand a bit more on how information is stored, organized, and retrieved from the mind.

Information Storage, Enhancement, and Retrieval

Incoming information or stimuli, which may be marketing communications messages, pass through or are subject to three

▼   **Exhibit 2-5**

Information Processing Model

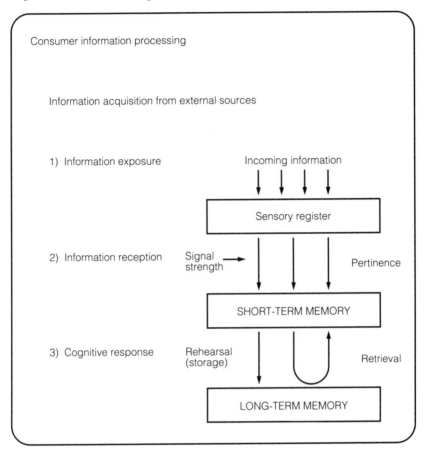

information storage systems in the human mind. The process is illustrated by the model in Exhibit 2-5.

As the model shows, a person selects information, sensations, or stimuli from the outside environment. The first processing step is the sensory register (SR). This system has three purposes. First, all incoming information whether auditory or sensory is transduced so patterns can be recognized. The person aggregates the sounds, symbols, and sensations into patterns that can then be tested against the concepts and categories stored in the mind. Second, the SR holds the information for short periods of time for further processing. Third, it alerts higher brain centers about the presence of these patterns so that the information can be further transformed and processed.

The second stage of information processing is the short-term memory store (STS). Information is held temporarily in STS while reasoning or matching takes place. (In the previous section, we called this the judgment process.) Thus judgments can be made about acceptance or rejection. Because STS is active memory, it has a very limited capacity. For example, few people can remember a seven-digit telephone number when it is first given to them.

The third stage of processing is the long-term store (LTS). This is the repository of all information that a person ever has processed. The LTS holds information that is not currently being used or that is stored by the person. We call this long-term storage system long-term memory or the mind.

Long-term memory, which contains all the concepts and categories that the person has developed over time, is organized in two ways, both of which are hierarchical. First is the semantic organization. Typically, this kind of information is stored hierarchically. It is illustrated in Exhibit 2-6.

For example, in the broad category of "beverage," the explanatory concepts are stored in hierarchical order. "Soft drinks" and "fruit juices" are made up of the concepts of "all natural," "diet," and so on. In each of these structures, the concept consists of several additional bits of information that enhance and expand the basic concept. These pieces of information are critical to the success of marketing communications.

The second way information is stored is temporally. People store information and events in the order in which they have occurred over time. Thus people can recall events, situations, or activities from the past with great clarity and they can put them in the proper time sequence. We call this ability to store and recall information temporally "experience." It is what enables people to change, adjust, and enhance the concepts that they have stored over the years.

Much more could be said about the human information processing system that is used to capture, store, and manipulate information. For our purposes, however, this general understanding of the system is enough, for it will help explain why integrated marketing communications is such a critical issue for the future.

The real basis for understanding any type of marketing communications impact is the concept of judgment. This process,

▼ **Exhibit 2-6**

Beverage Hierarchy Illustration

Source: Joan Myers-Levy and Alice M. Tybout, "Schema Congruity as a Basis for Product Evaluation." *Journal of Consumer Research* 16 (June 1989): 42.

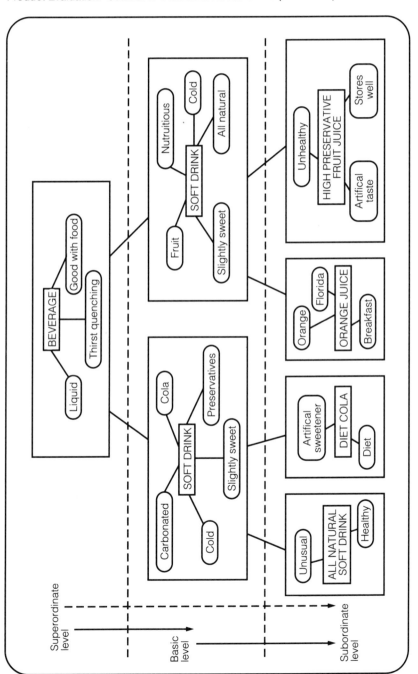

which a person uses to evaluate any type of new marketing communications information, is critical in understanding integrated
marketing communications. To understand the judgment process,
it is necessary to look a bit closer at how information is stored and
the manner in which it is interconnected in the form of concepts
and categories.

Chunking and Networks

As was seen in Exhibit 2-6, concepts are not singular units. They
are networks of concepts which are gathered together into what
we call categories. These groups of concepts are not only made up
of chunks of information but they are also networked together.
Some simple examples of chunking and networks are illustrated
in Exhibit 2-7.

As can be seen, the human mind is made up of a vast
network of concepts and categories that cover all forms of human
activity. Thus when new information is processed, it is tested
against these nodes and networks to see if there is a match or if
there is some sort of categorization scheme that can be used to
store the information. For example, when the concept of a voice-
activated computer is exposed to a consumer, the concept likely is
matched against the category of computers or telephones, perhaps
against voice and sound, and possibly even against technology. If
there is no network or node against which the concept can be
matched or there is no congruence, the concept of a voice-activated
computer most likely will be rejected. The person will consider it
as being impossible, a pipe dream, or not at all practical. Thus the
new information will be rejected because it cannot be matched
against existing concepts or categories. It is this continuing matching and judgment process that enables humans to learn and
expand their knowledge. It is also the process that marketers hope
to use to expand a consumer's knowledge about products or
services that may result later in a purchase or in product usage.

These concepts of information processing and storage can
now be related to our understanding of integrated marketing
communications. We can then begin to understand why the
concept of integration is so critical to the future success of all
types of marketing organizations.

▼   **Exhibit 2-7**

Three Concept Networks

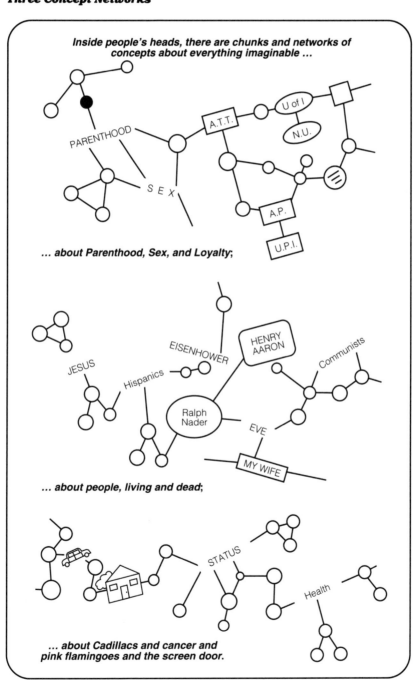

Inside people's heads, there are chunks and networks of
concepts about everything imaginable ...

... about Parenthood, Sex, and Loyalty;

... about people, living and dead;

... about Cadillacs and cancer and
pink flamingoes and the screen door.

Information Processing and Integrated Marketing Communications

As we have previously discussed, most consumers take in, process and store marketing communications information in a horizontal fashion. They accept information from a wide variety of sources across many media and in many forms and formats. Consumers use the same information-processing approach whether the new data comes from advertising, sales promotion, a salesperson, or an article or story in a newspaper or magazine. Thus marketers' products and services are subjected to the same judgmental approach of testing against retained concepts and categories no matter what the source of the information. If we understand this horizontal approach, four issues appear to be critical for the future.

Information Control

Today, marketers have a fair amount of control over what customers and prospects hear or learn about their products. They control this flow of information through paid and non-paid media placements. As the information explosion continues and the availability and ease of access to data expand, consumers will have more opportunities to gather information about marketers' products and services. Information may come from a wide variety of outside sources. For example, it may come from non-biased sources such as *Consumer Reports* or Underwriters Laboratories or from competitively placed stories, articles, and activities which consumers may access through Lexis/Nexis. Consumers may also get information from other database sources or simply from the increasing variety of media available to them. In fact, the most likely scenario is that the consumer of the late 1990s will access information upon demand or need rather than through our current system of marketer-directed and marketer-controlled message distribution systems. Whichever occurs, it becomes obvious that if the marketer hopes to influence the consumer of the '90s, there must be a clear, consistent message on behalf of the product or service no matter what the source or system. Conflicting messages, delivered through a variety of sources, simply cannot and likely will not be processed by the consumer.

Information Processing

From what we now know about information processing, the critical process determining whether a person will use marketing communications information depends almost entirely on the ways consumers test new product or service information against their existing stored concepts, categories, and networks. These areas obviously can be expanded and enhanced over time. However the marketer who presents non-integrated messages risks not having any of his or her messages processed because of the conflict that occurs in the consumer's information processing system. If for no other reason than risk of confusion, marketers must integrate their messages or consumers will simply ignore them.

Information Overload

As we move more and more from verbal-based to visual-based communication systems, consumers' information processing systems will continue to change and evolve. There will be more "sound-bite" learning. There will be less information stored about individual products and services as the marketplace expands. Consumers won't have the time or the storage capacity to learn a great deal about a product or service except perhaps from personal experience. Thus with incredible amounts of stimulation, limited processing capacity, and more concepts and categories to process and store, the consumer may move to broader categories for products and services. With this process will come less opportunity for products and services to be differentiated. Thus the message that marketing organizations deliver must be clear, concise, and persuasive. That demands the integration of all forms of marketing communications activities.

Relationship Marketing

As marketers and customers learn more about each other through various forms of two-way communication systems, the integration of marketing communications will become natural. In the coming age of one-on-one or relationship marketing, communication will become the critical ingredient in building and maintaining relationships. If marketer and customer do not communicate in both directions, the relationship will fail and the customer will drift away.

In a relationship, it is only natural for both parties to be consistent in their communications with each other. To build relationships with customers rather than merely to be involved in transactions, the marketer must integrate communication forms to build a consistent approach that in turn will build the relationship.

There is a final reason why integrated marketing communications is critical to the marketing future of all organizations. The reason concerns changes in our beliefs about how marketing communications impacts consumers. We deal with that next.

Replacement or Accumulation? Which Is the Right Model?

One reason integrated marketing communications was not considered important in the past was that many managers had erroneous assumptions about how marketing communications messages impacted their customers and prospects. Two opposing views were held and two models were used. Unfortunately, we may have used the wrong model and made the wrong assumptions during the heyday of mass media.

▼   **Exhibit 2-8**
The Replacement Model

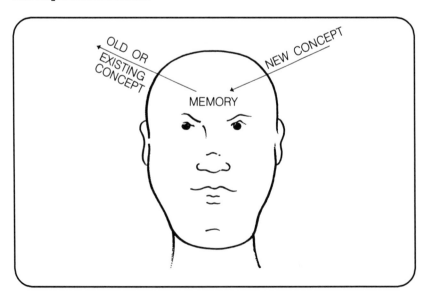

One theory of mass media communication effects is based on the replacement model. This model, which is illustrated in Exhibit 2-8, suggests that new marketing messages about products or services can "replace" those which consumers may have held previously. As marketers deliver messages on behalf of their products, these messages tend to replace the concepts consumers have had about the product or service.

As the illustration shows, many marketers believe today that they can blow competitive products out of the consumer's mind with the sheer weight of marketing communications messages. This hypodermic approach to marketing communications suggests that existing preferences, experiences, and even concepts and categories can be replaced by the messages the marketer delivers. This approach has led to the concept of "positioning" and the use of warfare analogies and metaphors in marketing management. The marketer, by delivering more messages than competitors, can "capture" the product category in the consumer's mind.

In truth, what probably takes place is a form of accumulation. The accumulation model is illustrated in Exhibit 2-9. The accumulation model suggests that information is not replaced; new information is combined with existing concepts and data. Therefore, marketing communications is part of an accumulation

▼   **Exhibit 2-9**

The Accumulation Model

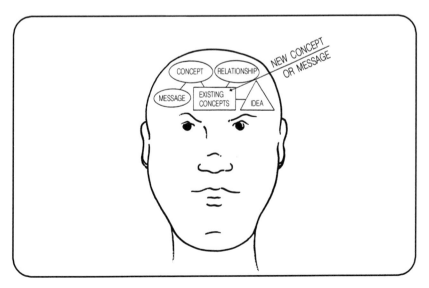

process through which information about products and services is processed, stored, and retrieved on a continuing basis. This model is much closer to our previous description of information processing as a judgment process.

If information processing occurs as we have outlined in the earlier part of this chapter, and there is strong evidence that it does, then the accumulation model is probably the correct approach to use in understanding how marketing communications impacts consumers. This further shows why integrated marketing communications is a must for the future.

If the replacement model were correct and the marketer could truly "replace" what customers had stored, then it really wouldn't matter what the marketer said as long as he or she said it long and loud enough. If, however, the accumulation model is correct, and we believe it is, then message consistency is critical as the consumer accepts, processes, and stores information about the product or service. As we have suggested above, the judgment model prevents consumers from having multiple concepts or categories for a marketer's product. That being the case, the demand and need for integrated marketing communications is not only clear, it is critical to success.

With this discussion of information processing and how we believe marketing communications works, we can move to a more detailed discussion of how customer relationships are formed and enhanced through integrated marketing communications programs.

The Basics of Developing an Integrated Marketing Program: How to Get Started

▼

As we have seen in the previous chapter, some basic principles apply to all types of human communication. Most of our discussion has revolved around information processing, how people select, take in, process, and store information and other material. This is critical to understanding how integrated marketing communications works in the marketplace. We now turn to how a marketing organization can use these principles and concepts to develop more effective integrated marketing communications programs.

At this point, one might ask, why are communications programs, particularly integrated marketing communications programs, so important to the marketing organization in the 1990s. Have things changed so much that our traditional approaches to marketing are no longer appropriate or effective? Or is it that communications is simply becoming more important as the marketplace changes and evolves? As we discussed in the first two chapters, both answers are correct. Traditional marketing variables such as product development, pricing, form and type of distribution or channels are no longer as effective as they once were. In a less developed, less sophisticated, less informed marketplace these traditional marketing concepts worked quite well. Today, however, the marketing mix variables on which marketers traditionally relied (a better product design, more production efficiency, restricted or limited product availability, willingness to take a lower margin on sales) have lost their value as competitive weapons. Technology has effectively made them obsolete. For example, today most forms of product differentiation can be offset or copied by competitors in very short periods of time. The traditional value of production experience curves has all but disappeared with the advent of CAD/CAM (computer-aided design and computer-aided manufacturing) and robotics. Types of distribution, location, and other channel variables are now easily replicated or duplicated by competitors. Market efficiency has improved to the point where pricing is a declining advantage as well. Most manufacturers and retailers have squeezed margins to the bone so there is little maneuverability left. In our view, what most marketers face today is a parity marketplace in which the only true differentiating features are either logistics or communication.

Logistics and Communication

Logistics, the ability to move products, services, or information in a quicker or more efficient manner, is the name of the marketing game for the 1990s. Those organizations which have mastered either just-in-time production, delivery, and/or inventory are those which are winning the marketing battles. Witness the success of such retailers as Wal-Mart, Toys 'R' Us, and Home Depot, or manufacturers such as the Japanese auto makers and electronics companies or printing and publishing companies such as Dow-Jones which have mastered desk-top publishing and the electronic transfer of information and material by satellite to publishing plants around the world. These organizations are starting to dominate the world economy. And it is likely that the impact of logistics will continue well into the mid-1990s.

But there is a limit to logistics just as there are limits to the physical laws of nature. Once the logistics are mastered, fewer advantages can accrue to the organization. Logistical excellence is a one-time victory although it may be a continuing advantage. So while we believe logistics will be the marketing battleground of the early 1990s, it is communications that will be the real opportunity for the mid-1990s and onward. We believe integrated marketing communications can provide a truly sustainable competitive advantage for the marketing organization. We believe it is an advantage that can be found nowhere else.

The New Concept of Marketing Communications

In a parity marketplace, the only real differentiating feature that a marketer can bring to consumers is what those consumers believe about the company, product, or service and their relationship with that brand. The only place that real product or brand value exists is within the minds of the customers or prospects. All the other marketing variables, such as product design, pricing, distribution, and availability, can be copied, duplicated, or overcome by competitors. What exists in the mental network of the consumer or the prospect is truly where marketing value resides. This is what people believe, not what is true. This is what people want, not what is available; what people dream about, not what they know that really differentiates one product from another in a parity marketplace. That is why, we believe, communications is rapidly becoming the major marketing force of today and certainly tomorrow.

If we think for a moment about traditional marketing, we begin to realize that almost all the marketing techniques and approaches that we have used over the years are essentially some form of communication. For example, the product design is a form of communication. A sleekly designed, electronic can opener does exactly the same thing as a hand-held squeeze-and-turn variety. Yet, by the design of the product, the manufacturer communicates a different message, feeling, or value. The same is true of the product's packaging. Cosmetics, sold in bulk in a brown paper bag, will perform just as well as those in a sleek designer case. But the communication is different. The perceived value is different. And the consumer communication is different. The same is true with distribution channels. Products sold in an army-navy discount store communicate different things than do similar products sold in a department store or specialty shop. In truth, all marketing is communication and almost all communication can be marketing.

One way to visualize the importance of communication in traditional marketing terms is to look at the steps in the marketing of a product. Then we can relate the marketing process to potential communication contacts with customers and prospects. That concept is illustrated in Exhibit 3-1.

If we look at the development of a product or service, we see that almost everything the marketer does relates to or provides

▼   Exhibit 3-1

The Marketing Communications Continuum

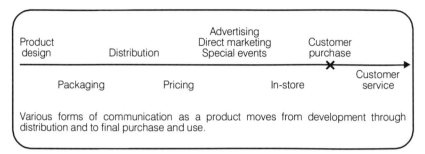

Product design		Distribution		Advertising Direct marketing Special events		Customer purchase	

Various forms of communication as a product moves from development through distribution and to final purchase and use.

some form of communication to customers and prospects, from the design of the product through the packaging and the distribution channel selected. These product contacts communicate something about the value and the person for whom the product was designed. It is obvious that the advertising, sales promotion, direct marketing, and public relations programs are forms of customer/prospect communication, but so are the signage in retail stores and the type of retail advertising done for the product. Even after the product has been purchased, the kind of customer service which is provided has a great deal of communication power among purchasers. In short, marketing in the 1990s is communication and communication is marketing. The two are inseparable. And for that reason, the proper integration of all marketing messages is that much more important.

Networks and Accumulation Revisited

As we outlined in the previous chapter, consumers gather information about products and services from many sources. They get it from advertising; from conversations with friends, relatives, and co-workers; from retailers and the media. They get it everywhere. And for the most part, consumers don't differentiate among the sources. Oh, they do factor in that information in the *New York Times* is likely more reliable than that of a weekly penny shopper. But in forming brand opinions and choices, the networks consumers form about product or service value, associations, uses, and quality most likely come from a number of sources that would be difficult isolate. Most consumers absorb information in bits and pieces. Then they put these together in the type of brand or category or usage network we described in Chapter 2.

The critical issue for most marketers is how to control the input of information that consumers use to build, adjust, and maintain the product/service/brand concepts in the marketer's category. It is quite clear from our previous discussions that the marketer has very limited control over much of the information and data that the consumer receives. There is not much marketers can do about what competitors say, investigative reporters report, or friends and relatives describe. That's why it is so critical for marketers to maintain some sort of control over the communication that they initiate or influence. Unfortunately, many marketers concentrate their efforts not on communication variables but on physical or measurable areas such as product quality, product distribution, and even pricing.

The basic reason for integrated marketing communications is that marketing communication will be the only sustainable competitive advantage of marketing organizations in the 1990s and into the twenty-first century. The marketer can control only a limited amount of the total information customers and prospects gather and process about products or services. Since consumers process information using a judgment approach, what the marketer says about a product or service must fit with what is already stored in the customer's head or is coming from outside sources. This, in a nutshell, is why integrated marketing communications is so critical for all marketers in the 1990s and beyond.

With this background on the need for and value of integrated marketing communications, we can now move forward toward the development of an effective integrated marketing communications program and plan.

Category and Brand Networks

The entire concept of integrated marketing communications is based on the way consumers store category, product, and brand information. As we mentioned earlier, this information comes from many sources and yet it all seems to come together in the same hierarchical way. An illustration of the storage mechanism consumers use will help.

▼ Exhibit 3-2

Hypothetical Beverage Category

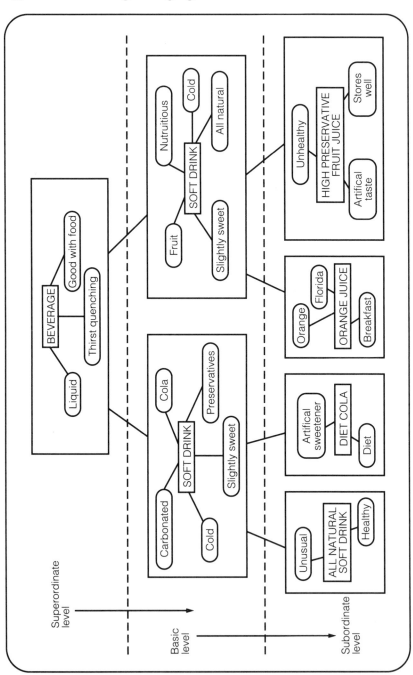

Figure 3-2 illustrates a hypothetical beverage structure that an individual consumer might have mentally stored away.

As can be seen, there are three levels of storage. These are illustrated in the three bands. Each band consists of a level of concept categorization that consumers use. Thus when the term "beverage" is used, this consumer would pull up the first or superordinate level of information. Superordinate categories are distinguished from each other in key attributes but they tend to share few features. The superordinate categories contain the first thing that a person thinks of when long-term memory is accessed as a result of some sort of stimulation. This level contains relatively little differentiating information.

In the hierarchical structure process, the consumer would then connect or move to the next or basic level of information storage in the category. The information stored at this level is considered basic because it is here that the concept attributes provide the greatest level of discrimination between categories. These are the concepts that tend to be used most frequently to categorize both natural and social objects. As illustrated, in the beverage category, this consumer distinguishes initially between soft drinks and fruit juices when considering something to quench thirst.

If the consumer then seeks more connections or enhancements of the basic concept, he or she moves to the next or subordinate level in the hierarchy. Here we see that a small number of attributes discriminate objects sharing a large number of other features. It is likely that here, at the subordinate level, most persons have stored or connected the brand names of alternative products. If we extend the subordinate category as we have done in Exhibit 3-3, we can see how this system works.

The critical issues for most marketers are where and how the brand is located and stored in a customer's or prospect's mental hierarchical categorization scheme. If only one brand is connected to the concept of diet cola, say Diet Pepsi, the consumer is likely brand loyal to that product. In other words, he or she will likely buy only Diet Pepsi whenever a diet cola is wanted. Most consumers, however, have a number of brands stored at this level. In our example these might include Diet Coke, Diet Pepsi, Diet Canfield's, or a private label brand of diet cola. We hypothesize that the goal of most marketing communications is to move the marketer's brand from the subordinate to the basic level in the

▼ *Exhibit 3-3*
Brand Connections

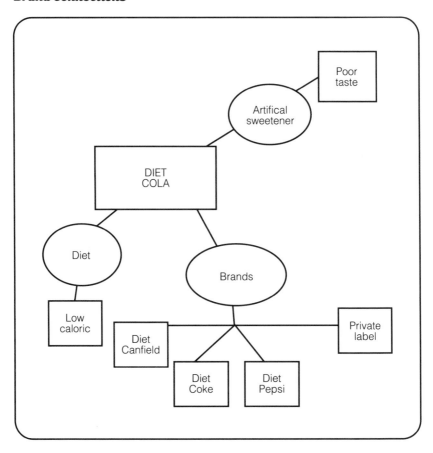

hierarchy. For example, if Diet Pepsi could be moved up and connected to soft drinks and replace the concept of cola in the subordinate level of Exhibit 3-3, then there is a good chance that Diet Pepsi would be thought of, purchased, and consumed, perhaps to the exclusion of other brands.

In addition to the brand connection shown in Exhibit 3-2, the concepts attached to the soft drink category are critical to the success of a brand. If, in our example, the concept of diet cola were connected to unsavory features or images such as "chemicals" or "bad for you," the likelihood that the consumer would select a diet cola when considering a thirst-quenching beverage would be quite low. Thus, we begin to see why it is important to understand the mental maps and networks that consumers have constructed in their heads. Only in this way can the marketer know what messages will make consumers change their networks or will reinforce the favorable concepts stored there against competitive messages.[1]

Contacts will likely be a new term for many advertising and promotion people, particularly in the way it is used in IMC. We define a contact as any information-bearing experience that a customer or prospect has with the brand, the product category, or the market that relates to the marketer's product or service. With this approach there are hundreds if not thousands of ways in which a person can come in contact with a brand. For example, a contact can include friends' and neighbors' comments, packaging, newspaper, magazine, and television information, ways the customer or prospect is treated in the retail store, where the product is shelved in the store, and the type of signage that appears in retail establishments. And the contacts do not stop with the purchase. Contacts also consist of what friends, relatives, and bosses say about a person who is using the product. Contacts include the type of customer service given with returns or inquiries, or even the types of letters the company writes to resolve problems or to solicit additional business. All of these are customer contacts with the brand. These bits and pieces of information, experiences, and relationships, created over time, influence the potential relationship among the customer, the brand, and the marketer.

With this basic understanding of category and brand hierarchies and networks, we can move into the planning phase of developing an integrated marketing communications program.

Moving from One-Way to Two-Way Communications

Traditionally, marketers have used only one-way forms of marketing communications. In the era of mass marketing, when the manufacturer controlled most of the product information that consumers used to make buying decisions, this system worked well. The manufacturer could select broadly available and widely used media forms such as network radio, network television, and national magazines to reach large numbers of consumers at the

---

[1] The concept of a consumer hierarchy is adapted from an article by Joan Meyers-Levy and Alice M. Tybout, "Schema Congruity as a Basis for Product Evaluation," *The Journal of Consumer Research*, 16 (June, 1989): 39-54.

same time. In addition, since product information was generally limited, there were few competitors. Further, a large number of new products were entering the marketplace and consumers gathered what information they needed from this one-way source. Since there was little other information available, this system worked to the advantage of the manufacturer and thus large national brands were built.

In the 1960s and 1970s, as products proliferated and information sources and channels expanded, the ability of this one-way form of communication to influence consumers through the mass media began to decline. Now, in the mid-1990s, it is clear that one-way communication is no longer effective in terms of trying to influence consumers. The media systems have changed so dramatically that two-way systems are required. By two-way we mean that the marketer and his or her customers are involved in an exchange of information. To accomplish this, the marketer must first know what information the consumer has. In turn, there must be some system by which the consumer lets the marketer know what information or material he or she needs or wants. The marketer can then respond, and so on.

In many arenas, this type of two-way communication has been referred to as "relationship" marketing. This means that there is a relationship between the buyer and the seller that normally results from interchanges and exchanges of information and things of mutual value. We believe that relationship marketing is the key to all future marketing efforts. It is only through integrated marketing communications, however, that relationships can be built. So while relationship marketing may be the buzzword of the buzzword 1990s, integrated marketing communications makes relationship marketing possible.

Enter the Database

The most successful way to establish two-way relationship communications systems is through some form of database or database marketing program. In this approach, the marketer sends information to the consumer through a variety of distribution forms. In each case, the marketers actively solicit a reply or response. Those response-solicitation devices may include a direct mail piece, a telephone call, a purchase warranty card, or other direct response form through which consumer then responds. Response information is then stored in the database. The marketer adjusts his or her communication program based on these responses. For example, let's assume that an airline sends a direct mail piece to a member of its frequent flyer program. The customer is asked if he or she would like information on air travel to Europe. The consumer then responds yes or no. If yes, the airline knows that the customer is interested in learning more about European travel and makes sure that the customer receives all future communication on the subject. If the customer responds negatively, then his or her name is removed from future communication programs on European travel.

In many cases, since marketers are not dealing with existing customers but with prospects, information about people may be gathered in non-direct ways. Traditionally, marketers have used syndicated research studies such as those by Simmons or MRI. These research organizations survey large numbers of people and then make projections about purchase habits, product usage, media habits, and the like. From this, the marketer can make some assumptions about a prospective customer's interest in a product or service. Increasingly, however, projections are being replaced by the use of more behavioral information such as that from actual customer purchase or usage. This type of information is commonly gathered from scanner panel information in supermarkets and increasingly from drug stores and mass merchandisers as well. Here, the store captures purchase data from each shopping household by means of an individualized shopper card and the UPC codes of the products purchased. This information is then shared in some way between the retailer and the manufacturer. Often some third-party data or research organization is often involved. In addition, various forms of consumer data are gathered from charge card purchases, from actual purchase data from other marketers, and even from some organizations that gather this type of data for sale. We believe that this increasing availability of consumer behavioral data is the key to successful integrated marketing communications. While attitudinal data, which is what traditional marketing management has relied on for years, helps explain what has occurred, the behavioral data really assists the marketer in developing an effective integrated marketing communications program.

▼ **Exhibit 3-4**

Integrated Marketing Communications Planning Model

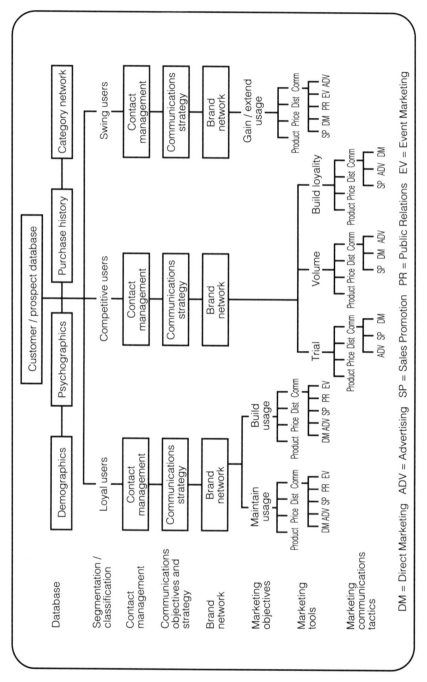

The Integrated Marketing Communications Planning Model

The basis for an effective integrated marketing communications program is based on the planning model illustrated in Exhibit 3-4.

As can be seen, we start with a database of information on both customers and prospects. While the database should be as complete as possible, we recognize that many companies, particularly those that market through retail channels, often have only limited information about their actual customers. This is especially true of large, high-penetration, fast-moving consumer products. Yet this type of information is critical to the future success of an integrated marketing communications program.

The planning model that we illustrate is idealized, that is, it represents the best of all worlds. Few organizations have reached this point as yet in database development. There are some, however, who have been gathering data about their users for several years. Tobacco companies, for example, have very complete databases on their users. Automobile companies are also building detailed databases on ownership and histories of purchase patterns. Direct marketers such as American Express, Visa, MasterCard, and financial organizations also have detailed information on their customers and prospects. In our experience, service organizations and business-to-business marketers are generally far ahead of consumer product companies in developing usable databases for integrated marketing communications.

As shown, the database should contain at a minimum such hard data as demographics, psychographics, and purchase history. In addition, attitudinal information such as the customer's category network and how consumers associate the products they use is vital for a solid integrated marketing communications approach. (Note: The planning form we have illustrated was developed for a consumer product. The data-base for a service organization would likely be quite different as would that for a business-to-business organization. We illustrate a business-to-business planning model in Exhibit 3-5, which follows later in this chapter.)

A major difference between the new integrated marketing communications planning approach and most traditional marketing communication planning programs is that the new focus is on the consumer, customer, or prospect, not on the organization's sales or profit goals. We push the marketing objectives farther down in the planning process. We are convinced that all marketing organizations are totally dependent on their customers and their prospects for their volume and profit success. The customer and prospect base determines how successful an organization can be, not how skilled the marketer is nor how many resources he or she has at hand. Thus no matter how skilled the marketing manager is, he or she cannot manipulate the market today as once was believed possible. Given the level of competition and the amount of information available to customers and prospects, the major task of the marketing organization of the 1990s must be to serve customers. The customer base really determines the amount of product that can be sold. To a certain extent it also defines the level of profit that might be attainable.

A second major way in which our integrated marketing communications planning process differs from traditional methods is that we use customer and prospect behavior whenever possible as our first segmentation approach. This ties directly back to the concepts of category and brand networks that were previously discussed. We believe that behavior more clearly indicates what a person will do in the future than do various intention or attitudinal approaches. At the segmentation/classification level, we differentiate among loyal users of the marketer's brand, those who are loyal to other brands, and those who switch from brand to brand. Obviously those who are loyal users of the marketer's brand have a different category and brand network than do those who are loyal to a competitive product. We use an understanding of the customer's brand network as the next variable in the planning process. This understanding can come from using behavioral data such as that captured through scanners, consumer research, or other sources.

The next step is what we call contact management. Contact management is based on the idea that finding a time, a place, or a situation in which the customer/prospect can be communicated with may be one of the most important tasks of the 1990s. In the period when there was extensive consumer-marketer communication and consumers were actively seeking information about products and services, it was much more important to determine what should be said about a product or service than it was to determine when the contact could be made. In today's marketplace, however, with information overload, media proliferation, and marketing communication clutter, we believe that the most critical variables in the process are how and when the customer or prospect contact can be made. The contact arrangement will determine what will be communicated about the product or service. We are not underrating the value of creativity in integrated marketing communications, we are simply saying that the conditions under which the communication will be delivered are as or more critical than determining the message content of the communication. For example, if a marketer determines that the best time to deliver a sales message is at a sponsored tennis match, then the message and tone of what the marketer communicates are greatly influenced by the setting. Some creative approaches just would not be appropriate for the setting or for the customer's or prospect's mood.

The next step is to develop a communications strategy. This involves the message that is to be delivered given the context (contact management) in which it will appear. In our communication management approach, we clearly state the objectives of the communication and what response is expected from the person contacted. In most cases, we try to relate these communication objectives to some type of behavior. This behavioral approach can be an overt act as well as include a change in the customer's or prospect's category and brand network.

Based on the communication objectives, we then define the specific marketing objectives for the integrated marketing communications plan. These must be quite clear and in most cases are quantitative in nature. For example, with brand loyal customers, the only real marketing goals possible are to maintain or to increase usage. If we wanted to maintain usage, we would have a quantifiable goal. If, instead, our goal were to increase usage, this could be quantified also. For a competitive user, the goal might be to

1   generate a trial of our product (this is a measurable objective),

2   build volume assuming a trial had already occurred (this, too, can be measured),

3   build loyalty to the marketer's brand and take it away from the existing brand (another measurable result).

As can be seen, this type of approach can be expanded as broadly as is practical in the segmentation process. For example, the preceding illustration includes only those customers and prospects who use the products in the category. We could just as well include other category segments for non-users, lost users, or whatever is required.

Once the marketing objectives have been set, the next step is to determine which of the marketing tools should be used to achieve the previously stated marketing objectives. Obviously, if we consider that the product, the distribution, and the price are forms of communication with customers and prospects, then the integrated marketing communications planner has a wide variety of marketing tools at his or her disposal. The key here is to select the tool that will achieve the communication objective. Commonly, most of these marketing tools are used in some combination.

The last step in the process is to select the various marketing communications tactics that will help achieve the communication goals set forth in the earlier part of the planning process. Here, the communication techniques can be as broad as the imagination of the marketing communications planner. We have discussed basic marketing tactics such as advertising, sales promotion, direct marketing, public relations, and events. In truth, there are many more techniques such as in-store retail activities, trade shows, and packaging. The critical issue is that each of these techniques must be used to help achieve the established marketing and communication objectives.

The key ingredient in this integrated marketing planning approach is that all forms of communication are designed to achieve agreed-upon objectives. These objectives come from understanding how we can contact the customer or prospect and what we want to communicate. Since the communication goals are driven by the behavior we want to change, adapt, or reinforce, there is no way any form of communication can stray from that task. We have turned all forms of marketing into communication and all forms of communication into marketing. We have integrated our messages and our goals. We have built a seamless stream of communication with the customer.

The Circular Nature of Integrated Marketing Communications

The real value of the integrated marketing communications process we have just described is that it is circular in nature. We develop an integrated marketing communications plan and then implement the plan in the marketplace. Since we have determined in advance that there must be some behavior on the part of the receiver that lets us know if the communication has been successful, we need to measure the responses of the groups of customers or prospects that we have identified in the planning process. As we are committed to two-way communication, we intend to get some responses from those persons to whom the integrated marketing communications program has been directed. These responses go directly into our database where they are held and can be evaluated. In the next planning cycle we know what response was received (no response can be considered an important response in this system) and we can adjust our next plan based on these responses. Thus we as the marketer develop communications programs. The consumer responds. We get information on the response. We adapt to the customer's or prospect's communication wants or needs and begin the cycle all over again. This is truly relationship marketing at its best. It is integrated marketing communications that develops a win-win situation for the marketer and the customer or prospect. This is what marketing communications must be for organizations to succeed in the 1990s.

Some Additional Examples of the Planning Form

Following are some other approaches to the use of the basic integrated marketing communications planning model. Exhibit 3-5 illustrates how a business-to-business marketer might use the approach.

Note that the major differences are in what is contained in the customer/prospect database and the initial segmentation/classification choice. Here we illustrate the segments as installed base of customers, competitive installed base and new/emerging

▼ **Exhibit 3-5**

Business-to-Business Planning Model

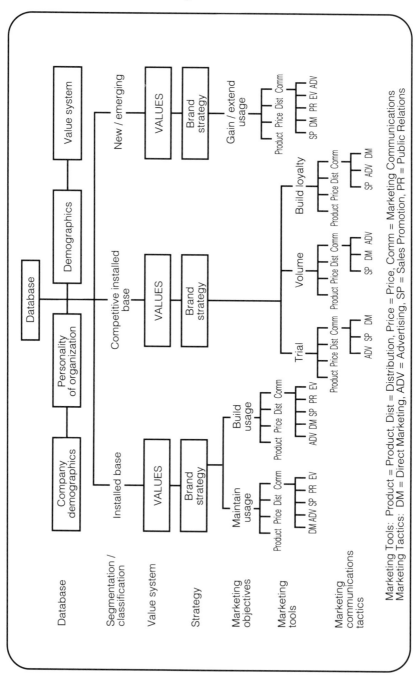

▼   **Exhibit 3-6**
American Medical Association Planning Chart

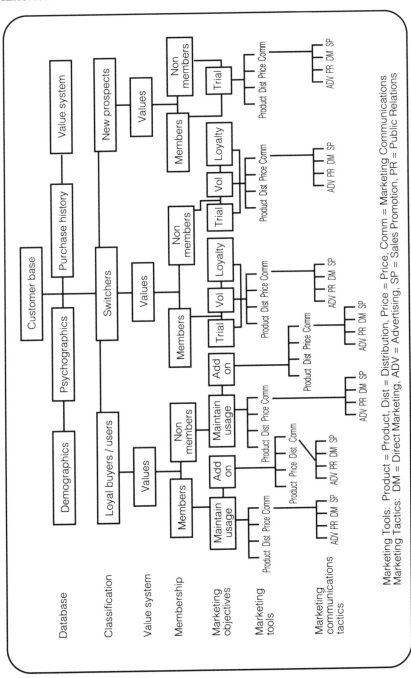

▼ **Exhibit 3-7**

Internal Revenue Service Planning Model

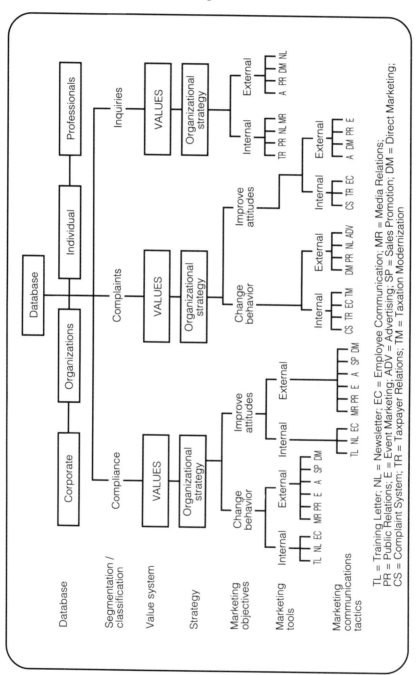

TL = Training Letter; NL = Newsletter; EC = Employee Communication; MR = Media Relations;
PR = Public Relations; E = Event Marketing; ADV = Advertising; SP = Sales Promotion; DM = Direct Marketing;
CS = Complaint System; TR = Taxpayer Relations; TM = Taxation Modernization

users. Again, the segmentation approach is based on behavioral activities of the customers and prospects in the database.

This same approach can be used for non-profit companies or associations. Exhibit 3-6 illustrates some initial planning approaches that were developed for the American Medical Association. Note the differentiation between members and non-members of the association. It is believed that the category and brand maps of each group are quite different. Therefore, reaching each group would require different communication and marketing objectives.

Finally, we include an illustration of how this planning model can be used for a government organization. This particular model was constructed for a group of Internal Revenue Service communications specialists. While the IRS is not a marketing organization, integrated communications is as much an issue for them as it is for for-profit marketing organizations. (See Exhibit 3-7.)

The Specifics of Planning

The conceptual model that we have presented is just that—a concept—until it is put into action. In the next chapter we illustrate a communications planning approach that will take its direction from this conceptual model.

4

Strategy Is Everything: Planning the Direction of the Communications Program

▼

It's a cold winter evening in Philadelphia. You're on Calumet Street between 13th and 14th. There are eight houses on the block. You're a door-to-door salesman. Your job? Knock on each door and sell each homeowner a bottle of aspirin.

You Need a Communication Strategy!

What Kind of Communication Strategy Would You Write?

If you want to be successful today, chances are you won't write the same strategy for all eight homeowners. A single strategy might lead you to say something like this: "Hey there, person, if you have stress . . . I have relief. And my product relieves stress faster." Of course you would need a visual to accompany these words, so you would stand there, with a pained look on your face, perhaps tightly twisting a rope to dramatize "stress."

One strategy for all eight homeowners? Of course not. But that's the kind of thinking taking place on mass TV today. One strategy, one commercial spun off that strategy, aimed at 70 million people. What this massification of the consumer has led to is vague, meaningless communication. Marketers spend most of their time communicating about themselves and spend very little time figuring out how their product can solve consumer problems.

The consumer is more than just confused about brands. The consumer is bored with brands, and he or she has every right to be bored with glittering generalizations jazzed up with show business. Most often what we see and hear today is communication that touches neither the head nor the heart of the customer.

The problem is compounded by the fact that most marketers send out a communication hodgepodge to the consumer, a mass message saying one thing, a price promo creating a different signal, a product label creating still another message, sales literature having an entirely different vocabulary, a sales force doing nothing but pitch "price," "price," "price" to the retailer. Mixed up, mass-directed, incompatible communication stems from the manufacturer's wishes rather than from customer needs. This is why we're in the era of brand parity and why we think integrated marketing communications is the necessary beginning of a new era in which the consumer calls the shots and the marketer listens.

A New Way of Thinking

Good communication—good selling—is personal. An effective salesperson would never ever use the same strategy to sell all eight people on that block in Philadelphia. What one should do is find out all one can about each customer and custom tailor the communication strategy to the individual. Get to know the customer! The better you know the customer, the sharper the selling message. Find out how the individuals on the block experience stress. When? Is the stress job-related? Lifestyle related? Is it real? Imaginary? Which products do they use to solve their problem? Are they satisfied? Do they enjoy using the products? Why? Would they recommend them to a friend?

Think how much easier it would be to communicate with potential customers if you knew them as individuals rather than as merely other guys on the block. Today's computer technologies make it possible to know the customer's needs, behavior, and media habits so thoroughly that you can address each customer on a more personal basis.

The Strategy Is the Thinking Process

This new way of thinking requires an almost evangelical dedication to the creation of a disciplined communication strategy. If you do your homework properly in the development of the communication strategy, it will result in a sharper, more persuasive—integrated—selling message directed to the most likely prospect. This, in turn, will result in the creation of a unique brand or service personality, one that separates your product or service from its competition. When done correctly, the use of an integrated selling message leads to personal communication, the kind of communication people want to listen to and to act upon.

This is quite a promise, but the authors have seen the process succeed time and time again. An integrated marketing communications program works. However, it will only work when it stems from a well-thought-out, probing, curiosity-driven communications strategy that begins with the consumer. The communications strategy demands creative thinking, the most creative element in the entire marketing mix.

At the conclusion of this chapter (Exhibit 4-13) is an outline of a communications strategy development form. It would be a good idea to review it now and refer to it as the text describes its various parts.

This strategy form is specifically created for an integrated marketing communications program. It can be used by blue-chip marketers or small entrepreneurs. It's essential whether you're selling package goods, services, retailing, corporate "image," or business-to-business products.

Don't be misled. It is not the form outline that matters. What is really important is that the form forces you into a disciplined thinking process. We emphasize the word *thinking* because you are not merely filling out a form. The form gives you a way to think logically. The communications strategy document is everything in the integrated marketing communications program. Written properly, it is short. It includes only a few pages that practically everyone involved will spend the time reading and understanding. The strategy helps the integration process work because the completion of the form compels all people working on the project to consolidate thinking in one document.

The integration strategy sets the communication direction for the brand or service. It brings the marketing department together because everyone must sign off on who the customer is, what the customer wants, and how the product will deliver. The strategy defines the position of the product, its personality, its competitive reason for being—and what benefit the consumer will derive from the product or service. The integrated strategy also states how you think customers will be influenced by competitive forces. Importantly, it provides behavioral criteria for which the marketing department will be held accountable. The strategy includes the best media (contact points) where the customer can be reached. It also answers the need for future research, in order to further refine and update the strategy.

Despite its specificity and discipline, the communications strategy should not be considered a straitjacket by the creative writers and art directors involved with the brand. In fact, it is just the opposite because it narrows the parameters of creative experimentation. The strategy allows the creative people involved more time to experiment and break rules since they are limiting their exploratory executions to one specific direction (more about this in Chapter 5).

In this new era of integrated marketing communications, the communications strategy is the imperative element in the communications process for all departments within the marketing organization. It forces every aspect of the communications process to reach the consumer in a unified manner, with one personality, one benefit, one selling idea. Every communication tactic that flows from the integrated communications strategy reinforces the reason why the consumer should believe in the product.

If you are selling aspirins, for example, all communication for the aspirins should be driven by the basic consumer need and should lead to the creation of one unified personality for the brand. However, the strategy can be broken down to reach subgroups of consumers like loyal users, occasional users, etc. Also there can be specific strategies against wholesalers, distributers, retailers, trade groups and all other peripheral groups that can affect the sale. Each of these segments has their own buying incentive and, as a result, the communications strategy will offer each group a distinct competitive benefit. This is true integration because your analysis of the customers leads you to well-founded conclusions regarding which group to target and how to reach each group. Tactically, this means that a public relations program could be the most effective way to dramatize the competitive benefit to one segment while still maintaining the basic brand personality. A direct marketing program may be more effective against another segment. A combination of all these disciplines may be employed against still another segment. The promotions to the drug trade, nurses, hospital purchasing agents, and physical education teachers may offer still another benefit but yet maintain the unified brand personality. The sales promotion technique must follow the strategic concept as should the packaging, the usage instructions, the logo—everything from catalog sheets to the sales exhibit at trade shows should have one look and one tone.

The pricing of the bottle of aspirin and the choices of retail distribution for the aspirin should stem from the same communications strategy. The combination of all these elements with one unified voice gives support and reason to believe the competitive consumer benefit. Every part of the communication mix helps persuade the consumer that the product will deliver the promise it offers. (See Exhibit 4-1.)

You can easily see the importance of the strategy. It is the key to integrating all the communications about the product— elements that affect everybody and everything that has to do with the sale, and repeat sale, of the product.

You can also see how the communications strategy can help break down the barriers in a company among various departments such as sales, distribution, packaging, sales promotion, advertising, customer service, and even research and development. The strategy can—and should—lead to total integration of the communications program. One person should be in charge of strategy development, but there must be "buy-in" from every function of the marketing department and even the CEO of the entire company.

When done correctly, the communications strategy creates a bond within a company and a stronger bond between the company and the various communication agents that serve it.

Besides determining the competitive position of the brand in the marketplace, the strategy should lead to the early development of an integrated selling line by the creative people involved. This selling line, e.g. "a little dab'll do ya," "Ford has a better idea," "The Ultimate Driving Machine," will serve as a rallying cry for every communication discipline. The line should drive the thinking behind every piece of communication. The selling line, stemming from the communications strategy discipline, should significantly differentiate the brand from its competition. It will give the consumer a good reason to buy this brand over others. One word of caution: the selling idea is not a meaningless phrase or slogan. It must be a memorable set of words or powerful visual

▼ **Exhibit 4-1**

Two Distinct Strategies Must Be Developed

The Communications Strategy

1. Pinpoints customer segments —based on customer behavior and need for product

2. Offers a competitive benefit— based on customer's buying incentive

3. Determines how the consumer currently positions brand

4. Establishes a unique, unified brand personality that helps the customer define and separate the brand from competition

5. Sets up real and perceived reasons-why the customer should believe in the promise of the brand

6. Uncovers key "contact points" where customers can be reached effectively

7. Establishes accountability criteria for success or failure of strategy

8. Determines need for future research that would further refine the strategy

The Execution Strategy

1. Specifies where and how to reach the various groups who can affect the sale:

   a. highly selective advertising

   b. targeted direct marketing

   c. public relations program

   d. sales promotion

   e. logo design

   f. product form

   g. sales, trade presentations

   h. distribution policies

   i. pricing policies

   j. displays

   k. packaging of product

   l. stockholder, internal communications

   m. sales literature

   n. clubs, workplace organizations that customers belong to

   o. friends, parents, associates of customers

   p. federal, state government regulatory groups

   q. after-sale follow-up: literature, guarantees, research

that dramatizes the consumer benefit specified in the communications strategy. It defines the brand's place in the market and the pledge that the brand makes to the consumer.

In summary, this is the beauty of an integrated marketing communications strategy. It will bring a company together to more effectively respond to consumer needs. By listening to the consumer, the strategy will lead to the creation of a motivating selling "line" that will sharply differentiate the brand from competition and thus build competitive perceived value in the consumer's mind.

How to Think through a Strategy

The first, the most important section of the strategy is the Target Buying Incentive (Section I of Exhibit 4-13 at end of this chapter).

Think back to the eight customers on the street in Philadelphia. Until you know how they think about pain relievers, how they use them, why they buy them, and what problems they have with them, how can you successfully sell them on your product? Of those eight buyers, one may already be a loyal purchaser of your brand, two may buy your brand every third time they buy aspirin, three may buy generic brands, one may never use aspirin.

The Target Buying Incentive

To create a thorough communications strategy, each one of these groups must be investigated. That's the purpose of the Target Buying Incentive (TBI) statement shown in Exhibit 4-2.

It tells you what people think about a product category and why they think that way. It tells you what problems they have with the category (or brand) and what it would take for a product to overcome those problems and thus make a sale. The TBI analysis gives you insights into the consumer's behavior and thought process. How does the consumer define the quality of aspirin? How does the consumer evaluate brand names? What does the consumer define as "value" in the aspirin category? Why does group two only buy your brand occasionally?

▼   **Exhibit 4-2**

Target Buying Incentive Statement

I. The Consumer

   A. Target Buying Incentive

          Product Category_____

          Group Number_____

     1. How does this group perceive the products in the category?

     2. What do they buy now? How do they buy and use the product(s)?

     3. Lifestyles, psychographics, attitude toward category

     4. Key group insight

     5. What does the group want from the product category that they are not now getting?

Target Buying Incentive: "I will buy a product that_____than any other product in the category."

   B. Recommend Target Buying Incentive Group. Why?

The TBI analysis forces you to develop key insights into the way the consumer lives, works, and plays; the stress the consumer is under at work, in social situations, or at home with children. Does the consumer get uptight when going to a dinner party? When making a business presentation? When going shopping at a fancy store? Is the consumer in management at work? Does her boss put her under extreme pressure? Does her husband? Does her mother-in-law? How does she use aspirin? How many does she take at one time? How often does she use them each day? What brand does she take? Does she switch brands? Does she have confidence in her doctor? In prescription drugs? Does she buy generic? Is she an educated consumer? Does she buy on evaluation rather than on reputation?

Which does the consumer have more confidence in, the product itself, where he or she buys the product, or the person who sells the product? How is the consumer affected by news stories? By word of mouth? By parents? By price of products?

This investigation of the consumer should result in a one sentence summary that succinctly states the TBI. This one sentence will state clearly what incentive or product benefit will get this particular customer to consider switching from the brand he or she is currently using.

In the case of the eight people in Philadelphia, you may have found that the group buying generic aspirins are terribly insecure about the entire category. They may think aspirin is aspirin and, with great trepidation, choose the lower price "non-name" brand. They may be uncertain of this decision and really wish there would be a brand they could have confidence in—even if they had to pay a little more for it.

This group's buying incentive would be simply: "I would buy another brand of aspirin if it gave me more confidence it was working better than the brand I am now using."

Of course, TBI sheets would be developed for each consumer segment in the marketplace. The information to construct the profiles could come from behavioral data, primary research, or hypotheses based on your own personal interviews, observation, or experience. After a TBI sheet is made up for each discrete consumer segment, a decision must be made on which group or groups would be most profitable for the aspirin manufacturer to pursue.

To properly plan the communication strategy, each group that can affect the sale of the product must be considered as a potential target. It is likely that separate TBI sheets would be constructed for retailers, medical professionals, the company sales force, corporate health offices, etc.

For the purposes of this example, let's assume we decide to develop a communications campaign directed at group three, those who are now buying generic aspirin but are looking for a brand they could have more confidence in. We now come to a key question: Can our product—real or perceived—satisfy the needs and wants of the selected TBI group? This raises two issues.

1   Is the current reality of the product good enough to satisfy the confidence needs of the consumers? Is there "news" in the product itself —facts never heard before—that would convince the targeted consumers that this brand is one they can be more confident in? Even pay more money for?

2   What are the current perceptions of the product by the consumer segment? Do they inspire confidence? If not, can new perceptions be created through communication in order to

build a strong, unique, positive perception of confidence in the minds of the consumers? Or are the existing perceptions of the product so ingrained in the minds of the consumers that they are impossible to change?

These issues can only be answered by conducting objective examinations of both the reality of the product and the potential consumer's current perceptions of the product. Let's begin part two of the communications strategy—the reality of the product.

The Product Reality—What's In the Product?

Too often communications people are satisfied with the superficial ingredients of the product. They rarely dig for news and find the surprises that exist in every product. Sure, we know that all types of aspirin have common ingredients. But this thinking leads to complacency. Look for information beyond ingredients, for surprises about the product that can affect perception. That is the purpose of the next part of the strategy form, shown in Exhibit 4-3.

For instance, how is the product made? Who invented it? Why? How? In how many seconds does it dissolve? How does it actually work? Does it work faster on smaller people? Does it

▼ *Exhibit 4-3*
Product Reality

II. Does the product fit the group?

    A. The reality of the product?

        1. What's in it?
        2. Why is it different?

    B. How does the consumer *perceive* the product?

        1. How does it look, feel, taste, etc.?

    C. How does the consumer perceive the company behind the product?

    D. The "naked truth"

    E. Conclusion: *Does* the product fit the group? Recommendation work faster if you think it's going to work? Why does it work? Why are most aspirin bottles colored? How long can bottles safely remain in the medicine chest? What happens if you take aspirins with orange juice? In a space capsule? Gulp them with a Pepsi? Where are the aspirins made? Does the munufacturing process need certain light or heat conditions? Who are the people on the production line? Do they care about you? Is the manufacturing process supervised by doctors, nurses, or epidemiologists? Who is president of the company? A researcher? Do aspirins work differently on different symptoms? Why? Can the consumers determine how many aspirins should be taken in a given situation? Should they be able to? Should the aspirins be taken prior to stressful situations?

All these questions—and scores more about the reality of the product—must be answered. Every party in the marketing department should contribute questions. What you are looking for are insights that deliver facts that are instrumental in affecting consumer perceptions, facts that could conceivably dispel the perception that all aspirin brands are alike.

Product Perception—What's in the Head?

As important as the issue of product reality are the questions of how the product and product category are perceived by the consumer. Although you have gotten information about this in the TBI section, we go into more detail here because perception is a vital part of the product. It is what creates the real value of the product. How does the prospect perceive the quality of the product? Does it do a good job for its cost? Does the brand name offer confidence? What does the consumer think of competitive brands? How is the consumer affected by news stories in the papers? By word of mouth? By retailer recommendation? By price points? Is the brand seemingly always on sale? Is it old-looking? Does the prospect trust the retailer? How close is the brand to what is perceived as the category generic? What does the label say about the user?

Most importantly, has the potential customer positioned the brand so definitely as a "me-too" parity product that he or she is unable to accept new information and thus make a change?

Now back to the strategic issues which were stated earlier: Is the reality of the product good enough to inspire confidence? Can this sense of confidence be persuasively communicated to the potential customer?

If research and good judgment determine that the consumer's perceptions of the product will never allow it to be accepted on the basis of confidence, then most likely other promotional tactics should be considered, e.g., price promotions or incentive purchases. If, however, it seems that the consumer's judgment system can accept the brand's confidence stance, a repositioning of communications strategy is called for and, perhaps, tactically a direct marketing or advertising campaign should be utilized. Of course, there are other consumer segments that could profitably be appealed to. These also must be investigated to determine which type of communication will be most motivational.

Using the hypothetical aspirin case, let's say research has truly uncovered a group of people whose needs are not being fully satisfied with products on the market. These people have stressful jobs—office managers, TV repairmen, door-to-door salespeople, purchasing agents, bus drivers. These people get bad headaches and dread the thought of getting them. They buy generic aspirin but they wish there were something better, different—something they could have confidence in and enjoy the secure feeling of knowing it would work. They would be willing to pay a premium price as they do when they choose brand name prescription drugs over generic. These customers rely on their doctors' and pharmacists' recommendations. They think their headaches are special and they need something special to relieve them.

If you properly direct your brand to this group of consumers, your product is no longer mere aspirin. It is a unique solution to a unique problem. If this solution is communicated effectively it will add to the perceived value of the brand in the mind of the user. It will separate your brand from all others. It will allow you to establish a long-term, profitable relationship with the customer.

Know Your Competition

Knowing your competition means a lot more than merely knowing about competitive market share and ad spending (see Exhibit 4-4).

▼ *Exhibit 4-4*
Know Your Competition

A. What is the network, the competitive frame? Why?

B. What do the competitors now communicate to the consumer?

C. How are the competitors perceived by the consumer?

D. How will the competition retaliate against your program?

E. How vulnerable is the competition? From whom will we take business?

First of all, you must determine whom you are competing against. What network of brands and brand alternatives are in the consumer's mind? Are Hallmark greeting cards competing against American or Gibson? Or, in the mind of the consumer, are they competing against the telephone, fax machines, or the U.S. Post Office? Or are Hallmark cards competing against short bus or automobile trips to mom's on Mothers' Day?

Aspirin. Is it competing against other brands of aspirin? Tranquilizers? Alcohol? Cigarettes? Vacations? Or special kinds of analgesics such as aspirin with antacid, baby aspirin, Tylenol, Motrin?

The determination of the competitive frame must come from the consumer's mind. What do consumers think about the various pain relievers on the market? What do they consider a pain reliever? What are the alternatives to aspirin, their pluses and minuses? Where are the consumer's loyalties? How are consumers affected by advertising? News stories? Medical reports? The conclusion of the competitive analysis should lead to the determination of which brand is most vulnerable in the market place? From which company will your brand most likely take business?

The Competitive Consumer Benefit

You know your customer, your product, your competition—now, what is the one key benefit that can motivate the customer to buy your product rather than a competitor's? (See Exhibit 4-5.)

▼ *Exhibit 4-5*

The Competitive Benefit

IV. What is the the *competitive* benefit?

    A. Must be a benefit—solve a consumer problem; better the consumer's way of life.

    B. Must be *one* benefit.

    C. Must be competitive—"better than" the competitive frame.

    D. Must not be a slogan or ad phrase.

    E. Must be one sentence. (See Exhibit 4-13 for samples.)

In this hypothetical aspirin case, the TBI segment has given us their buying incentive: "I would buy another brand of aspirin if it gave me more confidence it was working better than the brand I am now using." At this point in the strategy, the competitive consumer benefit should reflect the TBI's buying incentive. In other words, the competitive benefit should read: "Brand 'A' aspirin gives you more confidence it's working than any other brand of aspirin."

This statement of benefit—or promise—is what consumers have told you they want from a brand. The statement is directional. It is no way intended to be the words in a communication message (more about this in Chapter 5). The determination of the benefit must stem from the consumer. Is this what the consumer needs and wants?

Many people have difficulty in distinguishing a competitive product benefit from a product attribute or product feature. There is an important distinction between a benefit and a feature. The product feature is what the product does. The product benefit is what the product does for the consumer. People buy beautiful lawns, not virulent grass seed. For instance, a product attribute for brand "A" aspirin is that the product has fast-acting ingredients. The competitive benefit is the confidence you can have that the brand quickly will make you feel good again.

It is vital to remember that the key to effective integrated marketing communications is the solution of consumer problems —a consumer benefit that's presented in every media discipline in a way that's unique to your brand. Attribute or feature advertising

▼   *Exhibit 4-6*
Reason to Believe

> V. How will marketing communications make the benefit *believable* to the consumer?
>
>   A. Product reason why
>
>   B. Perceptual support
>
>   C. Communication support

—"how good I am"—is boring. The consumer does not care what's in your product. It's "what's in it for me" that counts.

The Reason to Believe

Okay, so you've come up with a consumer benefit—something the consumer wants and needs. How do you give the consumer a reason to believe that your brand can be relied on to deliver that benefit? (See Exhibit 4-6.)

This is the point where mere communication is insufficient. What is needed is persuasive communication integrated into every piece of marketing; persuasive communication that gently, subtly, credibly convinces the consumer that your product is superior to every other product in the field. This necessitates building a rapport with the consumer that is the result of a deep understanding and a communication that reflects that understanding. In other words, you must convince the consumer that your product will produce the benefit they pay for.

This type of confidence has been built up by Nike with its "Just Do It" campaign that displays Nike's understanding of the consumer and how an athletic shoe can make life a bit easier. See Exhibit 4-7. The real genius in communication is to figure out how to best persuade the target audience that your product will solve their problem. (Note that Nike does not show product features.) Should a traditional TV demonstration be used? What about a money-back guarantee promotion? A special event? Or is it language—the words and pictures you use—that reflects your knowledge of the customer?

▼ *Exhibit 4-7*
Nike Women's Magazine Ad

In the case of aspirin, can you be persuasive by sensitively identifying the individual needs of the consumer, e.g., a secretary under demanding pressure, a busy parent with two fussy kids at dinner time, a reporter on deadline, a pilot in a thunderstorm?

Can the way you reach the target—the contact—create the reason to believe? Will the persuasion be greater if the message comes through a personal letter from the president of the company rather than a generic radio commercial? Would the persuasion be greater if you talked specific solutions to specific problems rather than vague solutions to general problems? Would the persuasion be more powerful if you offered "news" about your product in a way the consumer has never heard before?

Whatever method you use to persuade—to present your reason to believe—it must be consistent in every type of communication from advertising to direct marketing, from "how-to-use" folders to the way the complaint department answers the telephone. The thinking behind IMC is that every communication—price, label, logo, promotion, distribution—should be created to help persuade the target of the competitive benefit. The greater the consistency the greater the impact, and the greater the persuasion.

Tonality and Personality

The meat of the message and the language—verbal and visual—with which it's delivered is important in building the reason to believe. However, the tone and personality that is created for the brand is equally important. (See Exhibit 4-8.)

The brand personality is not just fun and games. It is not a creative exercise for creativity's sake. It is not a design element or a cartoon for cartoon's sake. It truly gives the brand a life and soul with which the consumer can easily identify. It differentiates

▼ **Exhibit 4-8**
Tonality and Personality

VI. What should be the personality of the brand?

  A. What unique personality will help further define the product and differentiate it from the competitive frame?

the brand from competition. It gives the consumer a feeling of familiarity, a kinship, a friend. Excellent examples of distinctive brand personalities are Nike, Bloomingdales department store, the Marlboro man, Jack Daniels whiskey, and the Energizer battery. The personality created must fit the brand's competitive positioning. It must fit the consumer's perception and expectation of the brand. It must be credible. If you are trying to build confidence, the tone of every type of communication from advertising to labeling to coupons must exude confidence in its look, words, and attitude.

Would the selling appeal of brand "A" aspirin be enhanced with its chosen target group if a personality of a proprietary—semi-ethical—drug were created? Probably yes, given the confidence-seeking target customer. If this ethical type personality is to be created, it deserves repeating that it must be consistent in every way: the package, logo, usage instructions, pricing, retail distribution, advertising, and the look of the pill itself. And, most importantly, the communication must contain a significant message about the reality of the brand that gives the consumer a real reason to believe.

Communication/Action Objectives

A practical communications strategy sets out goals for the entire marketing department, and the principals in the marketing department should be held accountable for achieving the goals. (See Exhibit 4-9.)

▼   *Exhibit 4-9*

Communication/Action Objectives

VII. A. What main point do you want the consumer to take away from the communication?

B. What action do you want the consumer to take as a result of the communication?

  – Try product?

  – Send for more information?

  – Use product more often?

  – Other?

What goals should be set and what goals are truly measurable? One element that must be evaluated is the main message the consumer takes away from the communication. Is the message that was received what was intended? A second measurement must establish what action the consumer should take as a result of the communication. Do you expect the consumer to call for a brochure or the name of a dealer? Return a coupon? Attend an event? Buy the product? These goals should be clearly spelled out and agreed to by all the participants in the strategy. They should be monitored constantly. Obviously, if the goals are not attained, the content of the strategy and the various tactical components should be reviewed and, perhaps, revised. It could be that you're not in touch with the consumer.

Perceptual Change

A key evaluation of the strategy and its implementation is the competitive perceptual value it creates for the product in the minds of prospects. (See Exhibit 4-10.)

In this section of the strategy, the desired perceptual value—and how long it should take to be established—should be stated. The desired perceptual effect should be measured over specific intervals with the target consumer. This is a realistic way of telling if the strategy is working or should be amended.

In the case of brand "A" aspirin the desired perceptual effect should be to have the consumer think of the brand as a more dependable form of relief because it is closer to a prescription strength drug.

▼   *Exhibit 4-10*
Perceptual Effect

A. If communication is successful, (months/years) from now the consumer will perceive the product as_____compared to the competition.

▼   *Exhibit 4-11*

Contact Points

IX. Consumer Contact Points

A. To most effectively reach the consumer with a believable, persuasive message, the following consumer contact points should be considered. Why?

Customer Contact Points

Another key element of the communications strategy is how to reach the TBI group you want to reach. The answer to this, of course, is not necessarily mass media, which has too often been relied on to reach a narrow audience. (See Exhibit 4-11.)

The TBI definition at the start of the strategy gives you a lot of information about your audience. This type of information should be used as a "contact" plan to reach your potential customer. Where are they when they need your product? Where are they when they are most likely to accept a "selling" message? Where are they when you can be of greatest benefit to them?

Perhaps your information tells you the most stressful time for your customer is right after work. This contact could lead you to drive-time radio. It could be that since so much stress is work-related a direct marketing campaign should be launched against corporate health-department managers, personnel directors, office managers. If you are trying to position the brand as pseudo-scientific, perhaps articles on efficacy could be placed in newspapers and scientific magazines. Perhaps all of these media should be used simultaneously—with one consistent message, one personality.

The beauty of the integrated strategic statement is that it leads to tactics that may not be traditional but are certainly more persuasive because they speak to individuals as individuals. It's almost back to personal selling—that salesperson facing eight customers on that lonely block in Philadelphia.

▼ *Exhibit 4-12*

Planning for the Future

X. Future Research

   A. List types of research needed in the future to further develop the communications strategy. Why?

The Future

The strategy should end up planning for the future. (See Exhibit 4-12.)

What research should be conducted in the future in order to build a more perfect strategy? One year from now if all the recommended strategic changes are put in place, how has the consumer reacted? Has the consumer accepted the change in communication? Have they bought the promise of the product? Are they buying the product?

The answers to these types of questions will provide behavioral feedback that will aid in refining the strategy over the years. A sound integrated communications strategy is constantly being revised because the consumer is constantly changing. Your communication, your competitor's communication, non-commercial communication, new products, and changing lifestyles all make it imperative that you continually update the strategy and tactics used to execute it. It cannot be overstated that the consumer drives the strategy. You must establish a customer relationship—a friend rather than a conquest. You are not trying to sell a pill, you are tying to solve a problem.

Establishing this relationship, showing this knowledge of and caring for the customer, is the essence of what effective marketing is all about. In the past, marketing gurus have paid lip-service to the term "customer-driven." But that drive was mostly superficial. The core principal of integrated marketing communications is that the strength of your product begins and endures with the confidence the consumer has in it. However, since your product is virtually the same as your competitor's product, you cannot depend on the product alone to build the confidence.

It's the rapport, the empathy, the dialogue, the relationship, the communication you establish with this prospect that makes the difference. These separate you from the pack.

It is impossible for the authors to see how a brand can establish this intimate communication on a mass techniques basis. When you talk to everyone at once the message becomes so weak that it is a pompous monologue. Think of these empty slogans: "Heartbeat of America," "The Night Belongs to Michelob," "The Right Choice."

You cannot—*cannot*—set down an effective communications strategy unless you start and end with the consumer's point of view. (See Exhibit 4-13.)

▼ *Exhibit 4-13*
Integrated Marketing Communication Strategy

I.   The Consumer

   A. Target Buying Incentive
      Product Category_____
      Group Number_____

      1. How does this group perceive the products in the category?
      2. What do they buy now? How do they buy and use the product(s)?
      3. Lifestyles, psychographic, attitude toward category
      4. Key group insight
      5. What does the group want from the product category that they are not now getting?

      Target Buying Incentive: "I will buy a product that_____than any other product in the category."

   B. Recommend Target Buying Incentive for group. Why?

II. Does the product fit the group?

   A. The reality of the product?

      1. What's in it?
      2. Why is it different?

   B. How does the consumer *perceive* the product?

      1. How does it look, feel, taste, etc?

   C. How does the consumer perceive the company behind the product?

   D. The "naked truth"

   E. Does the product fit the group? Recommendation

III. How will the competition affect our objectives?

   A. What is the network, the competitive frame? Why?

B. What do competitors now communicate to the consumer?

C. How are competitors perceived by the consumer?

D. How will competition retaliate against your program?

E. How vulnerable is competition? From whom will we take business?

IV. What is the *competitive* consumer benefit?

A. Must be a benefit—solve a consumer problem; better the consumer's way of life.

B. Must be *one* benefit.

C. Must be competitive—"better than" the competitive frame.

D. Must not be a slogan or ad phrase.

E. Must be one sentence: e.g., "Sanka tastes better than any other instant coffee." "Holiday Inn gives you a better night's sleep than any other motel."

V. How will marketing communications make the benefit *believable* to the consumer?

A Product reason why

B. Perceptual support

C. Communication support

VI. What should be the personality of the brand?

A. What unique personality will help further define the product and discretely differentiate it from the competitive frame?

VII. A. What main point do you want the consumer to take away from the communication?

B. What action do you want the consumer to take as a result of the communication?
- Try product?
- Send for more information?
- Use product more often?
- Other?

VIII. Perceptual Effect

A. If communication is successful, (months/years) from now the consumer will perceive the product as_____compared to the competition.

IX. Consumer Contact Points

A. To most effectively reach the consumer with a believable, persuasive message, the following consumer contact points should be considered. Why?

X. Future Research

A. List types of reseach needed in the future to further develop the communications strategy. Why?

Chapter

From Strategy to Execution: Capturing the Imagination

▼

The promise of integrated marketing communications is simple: through the use of concerted communication derived from consumer need, you can build perceived value into your product and separate it from competition in the mind of your customer. If the perceived value remains greater than the competition's, the consumer will remain loyal to your brand.

The Creative Process

The success of an integrated marketing program depends on two distinct parts of the creative process. The first part is the strategy —"what the consumer wants to hear" (Chapter 4). The second part of the creative process is "how you're going to say it"—the creative idea that dramatizes the strategy. Both strategy and idea must be outstanding. You can't have one without the other.

The development of a strategy is a long, tedious reasoning and discovery process. There are no short-cuts to a good strategy. However, if it is not thought through and misses its mark (the consumer) it is a waste of time and money. Not even a great creative execution can rescue it. However, if you create a logical strategy and then execute it in a dull, ordinary manner, it is still a waste of time and money. Your execution will probably go unnoticed by the consumer. You never will have seen your money evaporate so quickly.

The Creative Person

The discipline of integrated marketing communications puts more demands on the "creative" person than ever before. The demand is to interpret the strategy and translate it into terms that will build a relationship with the customer that eventually will lead to loyalty to the brand, the company that makes it, and the stores that sell it. This creative person will provide the message that adds perceived value to a brand and distinctly separates it from all competition. This creative person, in our opinion, must possess rare talents. First, he or she must have the intelligence to understand the potential customers—how and why and when they buy. This creative person must fully understand marketing from the consumer's point of view. He or she must consider the consumer as a client, understanding that the consumer is tired of irrelevant messages warmed over with pseudo-showmanship.

The creative person must be curious about the consumer, the product, and the competition. He or she must not accept the advertiser's word about the market and then make ads out of habit or whim. The creative person needs to know the consumer inside and out before beginning to create and then must listen to the consumer for feedback after creating. The creative person is the spark who can make the difference between parity and loyalty.

The creative person's doubts and questions about the strategy should be respected. He or she should be encouraged to talk with the consumer and to listen and interpret. The creative person must develop insights about what the product category means to the consumer and how the consumer reacts to different messages and relates to different approaches.

Another burden that IMC will place on the creative person is to be more aware of selective consumer contact points. Getting from strategy to execution no longer automatically calls for a TV commercial. Instead of the big production television commercial, the creative person may have to spend most of his or her time developing a 12-page brochure, a unique wall poster, an 8-piece direct mail package, or promotions that cater to the target group's individual needs using relationship marketing. Is the best way to sell brooms through an ad in a women's service magazine or a PR event where participants get new brooms to sweep up a home for the homeless? The creative person will be asked to create new rules in the writing of product labels, invention of brand names, instructions on product use, sales brochures, and creation of trade show booths. The creative person's first assignment may be to write a 3-word headline for a card that sits on a supermarket shopping basket, to write a script for the store manager to announce a flash special over the loud speaker in a department store. As media gets more selective, the creative person might even have to do a TV commercial to run on a local cable station for the production cost of $350.

These demands on the new breed of creative person should in no way diminish the number one demand—originality. In today's cluttered world of communication, the execution in every medium must go beyond the ordinary. The secret ingredient that can eventually make or break a brand is brilliant execution against every consumer contact point—communication with a unique personality that consumers willingly identify with; visuals that stand alone to tell the sales story with impact; copy lines that dramatize the product's promise in a way that's never been done before; fresh ideas that excite you enough to get you to act.

Brilliant executions respond to real consumer needs. A need for product information, presented in an interesting way. A need for confidence in a brand, presented in a way that inspires confidence. This, in our opinion, is the ultimate creative challenge: to earn the consumer's loyalty by stamping out boring, pompous, pedantic words that say nothing and to replace them with meaningful messages that help consumers solve problems and better their lives. This is the way to build a relationship with a consumer. This is a way to build a brand.

The Selling Idea

Whether by advertising, sales promotion, direct marketing, public relations, the label, or the spiel of the person giving out samples in a supermarket, every brand and service must be represented with a specific selling idea derived from a consumer need—a creative positioning that defines the brand and what that brand promises the consumer.

This notion bears repeating. Every brand and every service must have a selling idea that positions and dramatizes the communications strategy. The selling idea should be imaginative enough to surprise the consumer and crack through the armor of boredom. Executed brilliantly, this selling idea does more than capture the imagination of the prospect. It establishes consumer confidence in the brand, builds a personality for the brand, and makes the brand a credible friend you welcome into your home. Most importantly, the selling idea's credibility and persuasiveness allow the consumer to accept the competitive benefit your strategy has put forth.

The selling idea can take the form of a cartoon character like Tony the Tiger, who leaves you believing one basic selling idea—"Frosted Flakes taste great." The strategy indicates that a segment of consumers want taste from a breakfast. Tony delivers that promise in a fast, fresh, memorable way. Tony is a credible, fun personality—someone you'd like to have breakfast with. (See Exhibit 5-1.)

The selling idea must endure, such as Black Flags' roach motel; or Miller Lite's "Everything you ever wanted in a beer. And less"; or Tide detergent's "Tide's in; dirt's out."

The selling idea will separate the brand from the competition. Repeated in every medium, the selling idea will create greater competitive perceived value for the brand and will enable it to

▼ **Exhibit 5-1**
Tony the Tiger

command high margins. It will make special promotional pricing seem really special. It wil enable the brand to spawn meaningful line extensions. It will build consumer loyalties that pay off year after year. After all, the selling idea really is a creative reflection of what the consumer wants from the product. When done right, it actually makes the consumer feel good.

This selling idea is not the selling of price, as you see in so many communication pieces today. "Price" communication is a temporary positioning of a brand that is easily "knocked-off" by competition. In our opinion, the consumer buying incentive among most consumer segments is not price alone, but the competitive benefit you receive for that price. That's why every communication, from direct marketing to marketing public relations, must be geared to delivering a consumer benefit rather than an ephemeral price advantage.

Where Does the Selling Idea Come From?

The selling idea starts with the consumer—the Target Buying Incentive (see Chapter 4). Then it grows from the mind and effort of a creative thinker who is given a sound communications strategy. Such a strategy for Kellogg's Corn Flakes might say: There's a group of people—older people—whose buying incentive is the nostalgic good taste of a cereal rather than the nutritional benefits so often claimed today.

The selling idea that comes out of a strategy like that could be communicated in a prosaic, dull manner. A great creative thinker and a demanding marketer will not settle for boredom. One creative mind came up with a disarming surprise idea for Kellogg's Corn Flakes. "Taste them again for the first time." The phrase dramatized the nostalgic taste strategy in a memorable way and specifically defined what the brand promised. Incidentally, Kellogg's Corn Flakes' market share increased significantly as a result of the selling idea. (See Exhibit 5-2.)

Does the selling idea come from the creative department of an advertising agency? The direct marketing agency? The public relations specialist? Or does it come from the mind of a creative specialist hired by a marketing communications expert in a marketing group? This is a difficult question. Its answer may signal the demise of the traditional form of communication agents and

▼ *Exhibit 5-2*
Kellogg's Corn Flakes Ad

services used today. The answer may result in the birth of a new kind of thinker, one who can put together a communications strategy that defines the customer, the competition, and the brand's promise. This same person may be able to convert the strategy into a dramatic selling idea that invades the consumer's head and heart.

The selling idea can be expressed with words, pictures, or both. It can use technology never before used in selling. For instance, Porsche recently sent out a direct mail piece to Porsche owners to rekindle their desire to buy a new Porsche. The Target Buying Incentive for this new Porsche is status, prestige. Did Porsche use a traditional headline? A prosaic letter? Feature pictures? Big logos? Phony status symbols? None of these. Instead, Porsche totally involved each prospect by sending a special poster to each person. The poster featured a photo of a Porsche with the prospect's name imprinted on the license plate. (See Exhibit 5-3.)

Imagine the surprise, the status of receiving a poster like this. Porsche made many friends. This was a brilliant execution of a sharp consumer-oriented strategy that started out as a direct mail piece to Porsche owners. In an integrated campaign, the individual name technique can be used at racing events, in TV and

▼   *Exhibit 5-3*

Porsche Personalized Ad

magazine ads, as newspaper supplements, at the dealer show-room, in the car manual, even engraved on the floor panel of the Porsche that eventually is purchased. As a premium you may even receive a vanity license plate with your name on it. Think of the dozens of follow-up promotions that can take place involving friends and family—all potential customers. This is an example of integrated marketing communications at its best: the strategic use of media in concert to bring home one core selling idea. It really works!

The selling idea can emanate from an exciting event which can be integrated into all media disciplines. Recently, Nissan employed a communications strategy for its Sentra car that responded to the target consumer's buying incentive of "a car they can depend on." (See Exhibit 5-4.) The selling idea was executed with a marketing public relations tactic. An event was created that had six "typical" Nissan customers drive two Nissans from snowy Alaska tundra to the steamy wilderness of the Amazon. Radio and television advertising portrayed the various stages of the event as if actual news reports were being made of an amazing happening.

▼ **Exhibit 5-4**

Key Frame from Nissan's "Alaska to the Amazon" Commercial

Direct marketing targeted Nissan prospects with news of the event's progress. Banners, give-aways, literature, and a personal oral sales pitch tied the whole program together at a dealership level. A totally integrated marketing communications program was built off a strong promotional idea.

When putting together an integrated communications plan it is vital that every employee of the marketing organization be involved. Your employees, your agents, your distributors, your brokers, and the sales force should all understand the intent of the strategy and the executional techniques. They should be invited to join in carrying out the program; they should communicate it to friends, family, and business contacts. This involvement not only adds value to the program, it brings a sense of belonging and pride to employees.

The Budweiser Super Bowl game played by animated beer bottles is really an integrated marketing communications program that emanated from a sales promotion idea. Budweiser wanted to get greater Bud distribution and display prominence at bars, taverns, and supermarkets during Super Bowl season. Thus the concept of the Bud Bowl was developed. It was a unique promotion that responded to the consumer's need for involvement with a brand of beer. Significantly, because of this involvement the promotion has received admiration of the retail trade, bars, restaurants, and practically every place that sells beer. The selling idea has been so powerful that even hard-to-please beer distributors have gotten behind it. The Bud Bowl has created fan participation in a fascinating Super Bowl TV commercial "game," a radio Bud Bowl game, and involving magazine and newspaper ads. (See Exhibit 5-5.)

This incentive promotion has done what a powerful integrated idea should do. It positively influenced everyone who affects the sale of Bud: the beer drinker, the beer purchaser, the beer seller, the distributor, the bartender, the waiter, the truck driver who delivers the product, and ultimately potential beer drinkers who watch or listen to the Super Bowl. It's a brilliant selling idea, rooted in sales promotion, that distinctly separates Bud from its competition by responding to the customer's buying incentive. Integrated marketing communications, it really works!

▼   **Exhibit 5-5**
Key Frame from Bud Bowl Commercial

Don't Settle for Less than a Good Idea

The director of communications in a marketing company should think beyond the mere process of integration. He or she must think first of the consumer and realize that most consumers are busy and bored, too busy to listen and too bored to care. They're tired of banalities and irritated by inanities. They zap, they zip, they snooze. They don't care about you or your message.

Consumers are weary of prosaic advertising. They question claims. They doubt everything. They don't even believe the truth anymore. Today's communication must take these facts into consideration. Absence of freshness or lack of persuasion can break a brand. Surprise and conviction can make a brand. Whether integrated or non-integrated, marketing communications is still salesmanship in whatever media we use. If the salesmanship is humdrum, the brand will be considered humdrum. If the salesmanship is exciting, the brand will be considered exciting.

The creative process is arduous. Great ideas aren't generated overnight or even over a weekend. They are rarely thought up on schedule. But it pays to wait. A sound strategy and a memorable selling idea can transform a valueless tube of goo into a brand that produces millions of dollars in sales. Just think of "Brylcreem—a little dab'll do ya".

It is up to the director of marketing communications not to accept mediocrity. He or she must understand the creative process and drive for a communications strategy and selling idea that are clear, persuasive, and provocative. The idea should not merely be one that works in all media. That is not the criteria. The vital criteria is how it is perceived by the consumer. Is it understood? Does it deliver the key benefit the target consumer wants? Does it separate your brand from the competition?

When you look at examples of successful integrated marketing communications campaigns or new campaigns in the future, try to evaluate them with the following questions in mind:

▼   **Exhibit 5-6**
Outstanding Selling Ideas

BRAND	CONSUMER BUYING INCENTIVE	SELLING IDEA
BMW	Great Engineering	The Ultimate Driving Machine
Wheaties Cereal	Nutrition	Eat What the Big Boys Eat
Marlboro Cigarettes	Macho/Taste	Come to Where the Flavor Is
United Air Lines	Good Service	Fly the Friendly Skies of United
Clairol Hair Coloring	Natural Looking Hair	Does she or doesn't she? Hair so natural only her hairdresser knows for sure!
United Way	Convenience of Giving	We're Putting All Our Begs In One Ask It
American Cancer Society	You Can Look More Attractive by Safely Staying in the Sun Longer	Definitely a 15
American Family Publishers	Chance of Winning	You May Already Have Won A Million Dollars
Apple Computer	Confidence in a computer	The Power To Be Your Best

- Do the campaigns make *one* specific promise to the consumer?
- Do they dramatize the communications strategy?
- Do they talk person-to-person the way people talk?
- Do they create a unique personality for the brand or service?
- Is the selling idea simple, fast, and specific?
- Is the idea a surprise? Have you ever seen or heard anything like it before?
- Does the idea have lasting power? Will it endure the life of the brand?
- Can the idea be used as a rallying cry for an entire integrated marketing communications plan?
- Can the idea survive competitive attack?

In Exhibit 5-6 are some examples of outstanding selling ideas in various product categories. They all memorably respond to a Target Buying Incentive. They are all enduring, highly motivating, and memorable.

The ideas are so simple, so involving they could easily be effective in any medium. IMC is a thinking process that works. But, beware. Don't gum it up with dull, uninspired communication.

6

Compensation: How Much for Doing What?

▼

As we've seen, accountability—"the dreaded A-word," as one worried advertising executive called it—is driving the shift to IMC.

But "Accountability for what?" is the critical question that must be answered before a discussion about compensation can even begin.

As the mission of company marketing communications (marcom) departments change, in turn so do the missions of its agency or agencies and many aspects of the client-agency relationship—prominently including compensation.

The role of the marcom department used to be "to translate the company's marketing strategy into tactics," according to a document from one Fortune 500 company's files. But the primary measurement of success, if any, tended to be shifts in awareness, perhaps favorability, maybe even preference. There was great faith that a lot of advertising produced awareness, which in turn led to favorability and preference; therefore, agencies were paid primarily to create and place ads. Period.

> A senior marketing official at a major industrial company observed: We paid them 15 percent for spending our money. Can you imagine the company rewarding salespeople on the basis of how much of our money they spend, maybe giving them a markup on their expense accounts, rather than paying them according to how much they make for us? And yet that's exactly what we're doing with our agencies when we pay them a 15 percent

commission on media and a 17.65 percent markup on production costs. Makes no sense to me. Never did.

But then our budgets were arrived at no more sensibly. We used a percent of last year's sales or an average of competitive spending, adjusted according to our market share. Incredible.

What's more, we felt a genuine responsibility to spend every dollar. We worked at it—sometimes feverishly, if the end of the year was approaching and we had money left. God forbid we should leave anything on the table.

Some marketers virtually have marketing communications recipes, issued as policy, printed and bound. A new product introduction might call for a tablespoon of press releases, two cups of TV, a pound of print ads, a brochure, an application manual, and a generous pinch of promotion.

Vendors are hired to produce the various elements, usually on a project basis. One manufacturer has a twenty-year database that its marcom people use to predict costs and negotiate prices. The company considers itself very progressive and prides itself on its purchasing efficiency. And so it might—except that the model of the marketing communications department as a procurement function is as dated as the straight 15 percent commission, which is now used by less than one-third of major advertisers.

The role of the modern marcom department is as strategic as it is tactical. Its mission is to affect behavior, not just increase awareness. The emphasis is not on things—ads, brochures, direct mail pieces—but on results. Its objective is not just leads, but orders—and profitable orders, at that. Money is not spent, it is invested—with every expectation of a tangible return.

Marketing communications vehicles are not purchased off a shopping list, they are designed as part of a plan to take a potential customer step-by-step over time from ignorance of a company's existence to advocacy of its product or service.

Where once advertising agencies, sales promotion houses, direct mail specialists and the like were dealt with separately (and even played off against each other), now they're managed as parts of a team and required to work together.

One agency search firm had an assignment from a major marketer to help the company find not just an advertising agency but the whole complement of functional partners. The overriding criterion for hiring a particular supplier was its ability and willingness to work with its counterparts in other disciplines, not its individual competence.

As part of the assignment, the search firm proposed to develop a comprehensive accountability-based compensation system that encompassed all work—advertising, promotion, direct marketing, even marketing public relations. This approach may be pioneering in its scope, but not in its intention.

Incentive Systems

More and more traditional 15 percent commission marketers are turning to incentive systems. In January 1989, only four of 157 client companies reported that they linked agency performance to agency remuneration. Since that report was compiled, however, at least 13 major advertisers have shifted to new remuneration systems with an incentive component—among them, packaged good companies such as Campbell, Kraft, and RJR Nabisco; automotive advertisers General Motors, Volkswagen, and Volvo;and other corporate giants such as IBM, Monsanto, and Scott Paper.

For example, one multiple-agency global marketer of food products implemented an incentive compensation program with the base commission set at 13.5 percent.

In some cases, division management grades advertising A, B, or C, according to its effect on sales. A "B" rating earns the agency the base 13.5 percent commission. An "A" rating kicks the rate up to 16 percent, yielding the agency an additional $25,000 on each million dollars of billing. A consistent "C" rating would be cause for termination. This system has the advantage of rewarding an agency for superior work, but it ignores the impact of promotion or other volume drivers, plus or minus. As the latter become more important in the mix—an inexorable trend—it will become more difficult to isolate advertising's contributions. In the next chapter, we will discuss how to measure integrated marketing communications programs.

In 1990, Campbell went to a 14 percent base, but promised agencies 15 percent if their work achieved pre-agreed brand goals (i.e., sales or profit objectives for the company) and 16 percent if those goals were exceeded. From the agency point of view, one flaw in this system is that client cutbacks in media spending can impact the potential of the advertising to perform.

Also, new product development and below-the-line functions such as sales promotion, client response, and public relations are still paid for via a negotiated fee, with the incentive for exceptionally productive performance presumably more work.

Another multiple-agency multi-national abandoned the commission system and production markups as unfair, and performance-based compensation as unworkable. Instead, management established cost norms for virtually everything they buy and negotiate annual fees with each service provider. Agencies are thus encouraged to be efficient, but not driven to overachieve.

Other Compensation Systems

Other advertisers are experimenting with virtually every imaginable variation and combination. Since 1989, 38 major advertisers have revised their compensation systems, resulting in 38 different schemes.

Guaranteed Results

Perhaps under the theory that "the best defense is a good offense," in 1990 DDB Needham introduced its own accountability-based compensation scheme, which it called "Guaranteed Results." This was the first agency to go national with a system that provides not only bonuses for aggressive goal achievement, but fee or commission rebates if goals are not met. The savings can be substantial— 20 percent above or below the base compensation amount.

To build a guaranteed contract, the agency and client work together to define exactly what the advertising/marketing communications campaign is expected to achieve. Together they establish aggressive goals and agree on how to measure the achievement of these goals over a specific period of time.

Importantly, the contract also includes agreements on the client's part to maintain a specified level of media support over this period and to focus all elements of the marketing communications mix—sales promotion, marketing, public relations, direct mail—on the same strategy, no matter whether DDB Needham performs these functions or they are assigned to other agencies.

Eighteen months after the announcement, no major client had yet signed up for the Guaranteed Results plan, but several had reward-and-punishment systems of their own, perhaps influenced by the agency's proposals.

Resource-Based Fee Systems

Arguably the most sophisticated compensation system so far conceived is one devised in 1991 for a worldwide marketer of high-tech products by Morgan Anderson & Company (MAC), a marketing communications management consulting firm that specializes in agency performance evaluation and compensation.

It is a *resource-based* fee system, which not only eliminates the haggling over what the appropriate commission should be, but levels the playing field within or among agencies providing the various components of an integrated marketing communications program.

It begins with an annually negotiated "scope-of-work" agreement wherein the agency and the client mutually determine exactly what the agency will be held responsible for—what capabilities, what services, what staffing levels, what work products, for what businesses in which markets. This multi-page agreement is extremely detailed.

For example, a scope-of-work agreement between a MAC client and its agency might specify under the heading of "Media" the countries where the product will be advertised; estimated investment levels for the year; level of understanding the agency is expected to have; client's requirements for quality control in the buying process and post-buy analyses; and, finally, what is meant by a "transparent billing process."

Under "People Resource," the agreement might detail the duties of a senior international agency person by naming the client executives he or she will interface with and at what intervals; specifying the levels of knowledge and authority the person is expected to have; even itemizing necessary skills.

"Defining mutual expectations at the inception of a relationship is often skipped over too quickly," says Lee Anne Morgan, a partner in MAC. "Later, people discover that there were different expectations, which leads to problems that may not be rectified easily. Establishing performance criteria, defining the meaning of results, and agreeing on mutual expectations between the client and agency is at the heart of accountability."

The overriding objective of this advanced approach to compensation is to develop an arrangement that is easy to understand, simple to implement, and above all, fair to both client and agency. This in turn will ensure continuity in the quality and quantity of agency staffing on the client's account and strong stewardship of the client's marketing investments. The agency will be motivated to do its best work for the client, secure in the knowledge that it will share in the rewards for outstanding results.

Once the scope-of-work agreement is in place, the other critical component of a resource-based fee system is, in the words of Arthur Anderson (the other principal in MAC), "mastery of *specific* agency economics."

To create a level playing field, MAC devised a comprehensive discovery process which probes in great detail such areas as the:

1 gross income received by the agency from media commissions and production markups under the old commission system

2 agency's cost accounting system and methodology

3 actualized billable time spent by direct staff working on the client's account

4 client's account direct payroll, overhead, and profit

5 agency's overall economics, including such miscellaneous expenses as profit sharing, discretionary benefits/perks, and new business efforts.

The agency's response is compared with Morgan Anderson's database that has been developed as a cumulative product of many such inquiries. If there are discrepancies, they are explained; then the client and agency negotiate a fee arrangement that ensures a fair profit for the agency for satisfactory work. The high-tech products company's agreement with its agencies goes further, building in a genuine risk/reward aspect:

Far exceeds requirements	+ 20% of base fee
Consistently exceeds requirements	+ 10% of base fee
Meets requirements	Base fee
Fair performance	– 5% of base fee (probable probation)
Unsatisfactory performance	– 10% of base fee (probable termination)

Requirements are established in the mutually agreed upon scope of work, and performance is evaluated according to seven weighted criteria—again, jointly established by the client and agency.

"The premise of the resource-based fee system," says Anderson, "is that an agency controls its own financial destiny through planned compensation for profit based on performance."

This system works regardless of the function. Advertising agencies are not treated differently from public relations agencies, sales promotion agencies, or any other provider of an integrated marketing communications component. In fact, one MAC client first implemented the system among its sales promotion and direct marketing agencies, then extended it to its advertising agencies.

Similarly, within a full-service agency the cost structure and profitability differentials between departments or subsidiaries no longer matter, because the agency's potential income is determined in advance.

Whereas the commission system prejudiced the agency toward media advertising, the negotiated resource-based fee system frees the agency to concentrate on results.

An obvious prerequisite to the development of this kind of system is trust. The agency must believe that the client is committed to the relationship, not just interested in chiseling down the agency's compensation, before it will discuss the intimacies of its specific economics. One prominent director of marketing communications who shares his company's strategic plans with his agency (sometimes to senior management's discomfort) says "If you don't have that level of trust, you don't have a relationship."

Lee Anne Morgan agrees. "A true client/agency relationship," she says, "requires each to assume 100 percent of the responsibility. While this may not work mathematically, it certainly does emotionally."

In sum, these are the drivers of compensation systems as they are developing in the 1990s:

1 less and less dependence on massive doses of media advertising to move a product, even by consumer packaged goods marketers

2 concurrent abandonment of the 15 percent commission, and gradually the commission system itself

3 more and more coherent management of all the elements of the marketing communications mix —integrated communications management

4 concurrent movement toward function-blind compensation systems, probably based on agency resource commitments

5 more and more emphasis on accountability, with increasing percentages of agencies' remuneration influenced by marketplace results

6 more commitment on both sides to work together, resulting in fewer divorces and longer, more stable, more mutually profitable relationships.

7

Measurement: What Did We Really Get from All the Time, Work, and Money We Invested

▼

As we have pointed out throughout this text, the critical difference between the new form of integrated marketing communications and the more traditional, functionally oriented activities that most organizations have used over the years, particularly those of mass media advertising, is that IMC must, in some way, impact the behavior of the intended audience. This is not to say that functional activities such as advertising, sales promotion, direct marketing, and public relations do not influence behavior. They often do, particularly direct marketing and sales promotion. The major difference is that IMC is planned, developed, executed, and evaluated with affecting one specific consumer behavior in mind, the process of making purchases now or in the future.

Database Analysis

The basic element that has allowed the development of this behavioral approach is the database. The database and the information contained therein are at the heart of IMC. The goal of the IMC manager should always be to know as much about individual customers and prospects as possible in order to better serve their needs and wants. This means the accumulation of data, lots of data, and of information, lots of information. The data are stored, examined, and evaluated through various forms of database analysis.

This process differentiates IMC from traditional, functional marketing communications. IMC starts with the outside-in view, that is, with what the consumer is doing or has done, and then works back to explain why these behaviors exist. The IMC goal is to develop communication programs that either reinforce the present purchasing behavior of customers or attempt to influence a change in the behavior of prospects in the future.

What Is Behavior?

Having said that IMC attempts to influence behavior, the logical questions are, What is behavior? How do we define it for IMC?

> Behavior, in IMC terms, is any measurable activity by the customer or prospect that either (a) moves that person closer to a purchase decision in favor of the intended brand or (b) reinforces the presently favorable buying patterns that already exist.

With a narrow view of this definition, many traditional marketing communications managers will likely say they are attempting to do the same thing. They develop advertising programs that try to influence attitudes. The attitude changes could result in changes in behavior. Or they contend that they develop public relations programs that distribute supportive messages for the brand or the company. This in turn leads to good feelings about the brand, the product, or the company, and this might well influence future purchasing decisions. So, they would ask, what is so different or unique about IMC?

The answer is fairly straightforward and it really illustrates the major difference between IMC and traditional marketing communications evaluation. What differentiates IMC from more traditional, functionally-oriented marketing communications programs is where you start in the measurement process, at the beginning or at the end.

The Big Difference in Measurement Concepts

Traditionally, marketing communications managers have used a concept of communication effects that looks something like the one illustrated in Exhibit 7-1.

▼ *Exhibit 7-1*

Hierarchy of Effects Model

Source: Robert J. Lavidge and Gary A. Steiner, *Journal of Marketing* (October 1961): 61.

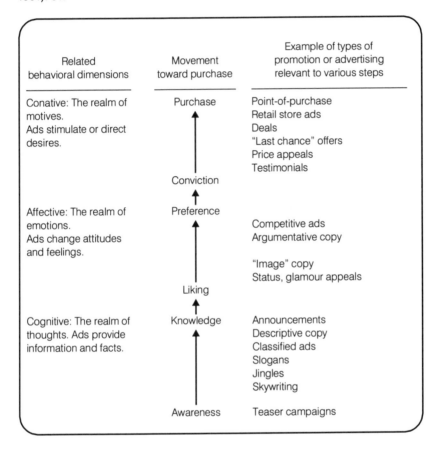

Most communications managers today start at what they perceive to be the beginning of the communication process—message delivery—and what they believe is the process of forming attitudes. Message delivery and attitude formation lead, they propose, to knowledge, preference, conviction, and then, hopefully, to some form of behavior. In the case of marketing communications, consumers are led to purchase or repurchase. This basic model has been formalized in the advertising field as the "Hierarchy of Effects" model developed by Lavidge and Steiner in the mid-1960s.

We've stylized the hierarchy of effects model in Exhibit 7-2 to illustrate the basic assumptions which support it. As our model shows, this is a one-way, linear approach to communications; that is, the marketer sends out messages, hopes they are received, and then tries to measure their effects. The marketing communications manager usually assumes that his or her communications message is responsible for any change in the communication process (i.e., the communication occurs in a sanitary world where only the marketer's message is seen or heard). In addition, the functional communications manager assumes his or her messages will move the consumer through the process. Finally, in most cases little or no effort is made to measure the actual behavior that occurs as a result of the communications program.

This model of communication effects was developed in the early 1930s and 1940s by communication researchers who had little way of measuring the actual impact of marketing communications messages. Markets were so diffused, channels so complex, and technology and measurement instruments so crude that only broad approximations of behavior, generally in a very aggregated form, were possible. These were largely best guesses and estimates. Since the research community couldn't measure behavior, it did the next best thing; it measured what it could—in this case,

▼   **Exhibit 7-2**

Traditional, Functional Communications Approaches to Marketing Communication Measurement

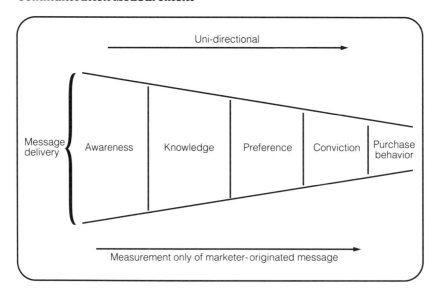

attitudes, opinions, and knowledge. Then it projected these beliefs into expected future behaviors. Sometimes the researchers were right, but often they were wrong.

Technology Changes the Game

Today we can, in many cases, measure actual consumer behavior in the marketplace through scanner panels, electronic marketing, two-way communication channels, and advanced direct marketing techniques. Therefore, while it has always been the goal of marketing communications managers to measure actual customer purchase behavior, it is technology that has made IMC possible. With this technology has come the need to rethink and re-analyze the results and impact of marketing communications programs.

In IMC, the goal is to get as close as possible to actual purchase behavior. Thus we start at the other end of the communications "hierarchy of effects," with behavior. Then we try to explain that behavior as a result of communication exposure which resulted in attitude, brand, or category network changes. Exhibit 7-3 illustrates the concept.

In IMC, we start with the actual purchase behavior. We call this a transaction. This identifies who our customers are and how important they are to us. (The transaction process can also give us our first cut at segmentation illustrated in Chapter 3). If actual purchase behavior cannot be measured, we examine some measurable commitment the consumer might have made such as visiting

▼ **Exhibit 7-3**

The IMC View of Communication Measurement

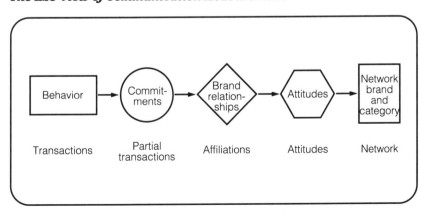

a dealer, writing for a brochure, or calling an 800 number for more information. We call this a *partial transaction*. No purchase may have occurred, but there is some evidence that the intended consumer has done something to indicate interest in the product or service. In essence, the consumer has "held up his hand" in one way or another to signify an interest. If a partial transaction cannot be measured, we fall back to the next level of behavior, *brand relationship*. In a brand relationship, we can measure some relationship or past affiliation the customer may have had with the brand or the category. This might include being a former brand user, being a user in the overall product category, or having an affiliation with the brand or category such as being a new mother, a tea drinker, or a member of a skydiving club. Our belief is that if there is some relationship with the brand or category that identifies the person as a legitimate purchase prospect, then some deeper relationship can be developed with the brand.

If there is no measurable relationship with the customer, the next move back up the purchasing activity process would be to attitudes. If we understand the prospect's attitudes, we might be able to explain some of the preceding behaviors or non-behaviors. The last measurement attempt is to understand the brand and category networks that the customer has developed that relate to the brand being marketed.

As one can see from this process, the goal is to measure behavior that is as close to actual purchase behavior as possible, wherever that might be along the purchase continuum. In other words, in IMC we attempt to explain measurable behavior by the use of attitudes, opinions, and mental relationships, not the other way around. Only in this way can we build the database and continuously improve our future marketing communications efforts.

A Circular Process

The other major difference between IMC measurement and that of traditional one-way, linear mass communication/mass media programs is that the behavior of the customer/prospect is a vital ingredient in developing the next wave of integrated marketing communications programs. That is illustrated in Exhibit 7-4.

▼   *Exhibit 7-4*
IMC Circular Model of Communication

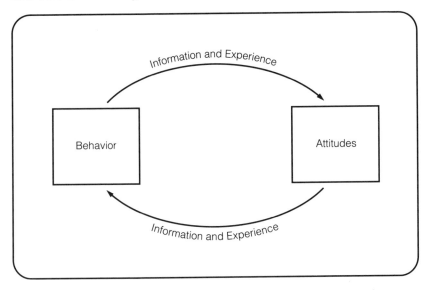

We believe that marketing communications is a circular, not a linear process. Attitudes no doubt influence behavior, but by the same token, behavior influences attitudes. If a person has a good experience with a brand, the experience either reinforces the positive network that existed before or it caused the consumer to change the previous network and attitude. It is this circular nature of IMC that truly differentiates it from traditional, functional marketing communications programs. With the circular concept of IMC, we can now expand our measurement model to illustrate how integrated marketing communications programs should be measured.

The IMC Measurement Process

The measurement process for IMC is quite straightforward. We attempt to measure behavior that is as close to actual purchase behavior as possible. In our measurement model, this means we would start with actual purchase behavior and move back up the purchase decision/behavior model until we could find measurable points. Further, the model says that measurement concepts should be built into the planning process. Thus when we develop an IMC plan, we would initially define the brand contact that was to be made. From that, we would define what was supposed to happen as a result of the brand contact. If the contact with the product were through direct marketing, an actual purchase might be the measurable behavior. If it were an event or sponsorship, the attendance at the event would be the measurable outcome. If the IMC program called for television advertising, the objective might be a change in attitudes or brand network, and so on.

The real value of IMC is that the behavioral objective is set in advance and therefore the measurement system is built into the process. The measurement is not an add-on or an afterthought. With measurable behaviors set in advance, the IMC manager understands that the behavior will be used to initiate the next phase of the communication process. For example, if the goal of the IMC program were to encourage prospective vacation condominium owners to send for a descriptive brochure, then the next phase of the communication/relationship building/purchasing process would be based on the information contained in the brochure. This is what we mean by the circular nature of the IMC process. With this conceptual understanding of how the IMC measurement process works, we can now look at how measurement and evaluation programs can be developed.

Measuring Integrated Marketing Communications

One of the major issues in the development of an integrated marketing communications program is the expansion of the concept of communications. We believe that a very broad view of communications must be taken. In truth, every contact a consumer or prospect has with a product or service is a form of communication. This may range from the design of the packaging to the way the product is displayed in a retail store to a rating in *Consumer Reports* magazine. In some instances, these forms of communication are under the control of the marketer. For example, the marketer can generally control product design, packaging, pricing, distribution, or where or how the product is sold or distributed. Obviously, the marketer can control his or her own advertising, sales promotion, and direct marketing. These are givens. There are many other communications elements, however, over which the marketer has little or no control, such as what is reported in the media about the product, what friends tell each other, what competitors do, or even, in many cases, how the retailer may display or store the product or the actual experience the consumer has with the product. The key to a successful integrated marketing communications program is knowing which communications elements can be controlled and which can't. The skill of the marketer then comes into play when he or she uses integrated marketing communications to

1   offset unfavorable or undesirable communication about the product or service or

2   to enhance favorable communication. As an illustration of this concept, Exhibit 7-5 gives a partial listing of controllable and uncontrollable types and forms of communication about a consumer product.

The first rule of IMC measurement is that a very broad view of communications must be taken. This, in itself, changes how one thinks about the measurement of communications effects, for it says that the tools to be used most likely must be different from those we have used in the past.

▼   Exhibit 7-5
Controllable and Uncontrollable Communications

Controllable communications	Uncontrollable communications
Marketer's advertising	Competitor's advertising
Marketer's sales promotion	Competitor's sales promotion
Marketer's public relations	Competitor's public relations
Marketer's direct marketing	Competitor's direct marketing
Packaging	Retailer's signage
Sales force presentations	Retailer's display
Events	Media evaluations and reports
800 and 900 numbers	Consumer comments
Company customer service	Friends' and relatives' reports
	Users' experiences
	Retailer customer service

Two New Measures in IMC

Traditionally, most advertising and marketing communications measures have attempted to isolate the communication message or technique and measure its effect. For example, many mass communications measures are based on the concept of a pre-post testing system. A measurement is taken of a person's awareness, recall, or knowledge prior to the implementation of the communications program. Then the communications message is delivered. Following that, another reading of awareness, recall, or knowledge is taken. The premise is that the communications program or the message was responsible for the awareness, knowledge, or recall changes. While this is a fairly standard research technique, it ignores two issues that we believe are vital in measuring the effects of integrated marketing communications programs.

Measurement over Time

As was previously discussed, there is little question that the marketplace is dynamic, as are the brand networks which consumers create in their minds. Most traditional advertising and marketing communications research approaches measure only a single point in time, i.e., when the communication was delivered or shortly thereafter. We strongly believe that the real value of integrated marketing communications is the effect of a planned communications program emanating from a database over time. Thus, there is a need to look at how the communications programs impact the behavior of customers and prospects at several points in a period of time. That means knowing the communication history of the customer or prospect in addition to knowing what messages the marketer delivered.

Multidimensional Measures

Traditionally, one-way communications measurement techniques have been designed to measure only the effect or impact of that communication tool or the result that particular communication message had on attitudes, awareness and so on. Integrated marketing communications assumes that there will likely be multiple messages, some controlled and some uncontrolled, that will influence a consumer's behavior. Therefore, we believe that the measurement of communications effects must be multidimensional. We must measure the behavior and the communication and then try to separate the two. While this substantially complicates the measurement techniques and requirements, it is a critical step in really understanding how integrated marketing communications might have impacted the consumer's behavior.

Forms of Behavior

Having said that IMC must impact behavior, we must also redefine consumer behavior. Traditionally, marketers have defined consumer behavior as how consumers act and react in the marketplace. Often, very narrow definitions of consumer behavior have been developed. We use a somewhat broader approach.

We believe that consumer behavior, as it relates to integrated marketing communications, might be classified in four ways. Each of these can be used in the evaluation of IMC effects. This is illustrated in Exhibit 7-6.

Transactions

These are measurable consumer actions, generally in the form of making purchases or leases, or other ways in which the acceptance of the marketer's offer is confirmed. For example, a transaction would include the consumer's purchase of a product when the marketer has some record of that activity. A transaction might also include such things as the use of an American Express

▼   *Exhibit 7-6*
IMC Communication Effects Model

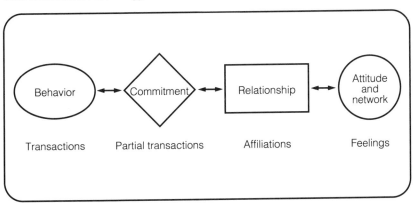

charge card, renewal of an Allstate insurance policy, frequenting the same barber or beauty shop regularly, or even the use of AT&T long distance service. The key ingredients are that the behavior is favorable and measurable and that it can be related to the specific consumer who has responded.

Partial Transactions

Partial transactions are those activities in which a consumer signifies some affiliation or association with the marketing organization but not in the form of a transaction. This might include a consumer calling an 800 number for more information, seeing a dealer, sending in a coupon for a brochure, and other similar actions which do not result specifically in a transaction. The concept of partial transactions is wide-ranging and will likely be different for each marketing organization depending on how it views the purchasing process. No matter what the form, the result is the same— a specific, measurable behavior by the consumer in response to the marketer's integrated marketing communications program.

Relationship

We classify activities that are not directly measurable as transactions or partial transactions as relationships. Relationships exist in the marketplace when the marketer and the ultimate consumer may not have direct contact. For example, the makers of M&M's candies have relationships with millions of consumers around the world. Yet the candy's manufacturer might never have any direct transactions with the ultimate consumers. The reason? M&M's uses a wide variety of retail trade channels. Thus the customer conducts a transaction with the supermarket, the drug store, the candy shop, or wherever else M&M's are sold. The customers technically are not customers of M&M's since they buy from some type of retailer. Yet these people do have a relationship with M&M's just as if they had bought directly. M&M's therefore wants to build and maintain that relationship even if it is from a distance. The best way to measure relationship is through the brand network that the consumer has constructed about M&M's.

In addition, we might classify as relationships the affiliations that consumers have with related or allied product categories. For example, a person owns a motorboat. Although the individual might not have any purchase record of swimsuits, boat ownership has created some sort of affiliation or relationship with swimsuit manufacturers. The same is true for dog owners and dog food or railroad commuters and newspaper publishers. Where there is category usage, there should be some sort of relationship between the brand manufacturer and the consumer.

Attitudes

As we discussed in Chapter 3, every person stores information in the form of mental nodes and networks. These networks are dynamic and are constantly being adjusted and enhanced as a result of new information with which the consumer comes in contact. As a result of these contacts, networks are formed that generate attitudes. These networks may result in the creation of the feelings and beliefs we have about products and services. We call these feelings and beliefs "attitudes."

It is possible to measure attitudes at any one point in time. But because networks and attitudes are dynamic, they are accurate only for that *one* point in time. Thus while attitude measurement is widely used in traditional marketing communications management, it is only of use in trying to understand behavior over time in IMC. It is likely that attitudes do result in behavior at some level. The problem is that when we measure attitudes, we really don't know how or if they will be used when it comes time to make a purchasing decision.

We can, however, classify attitudes as a form of behavior. That is, the consumer is not born with attitudes about certain products, brands, or situations. These are formed over time, generally through some type of external communication. Therefore, if the consumer changes his attitude about a product or service as a result of a marketer's integrated marketing communications program, we could call that change a behavior. The consumer has changed the network and therefore the attitude toward a brand or product based on information or communication.

With this classification scheme, we can start to develop approaches for measuring the behavioral response to marketing communications programs. Our next question is: What to measure?

What to Measure

Through our planning model we have developed a method of evaluation that can serve as the basis for our measurement system. Since our planning model is built on behavioral segmentation, which comes from a database, it is only natural that we should be measuring behavioral responses which can then flow back into the database. As we described earlier, the planning process is circular in nature. First we develop market segments from the database. Then we develop marketing communications programs to reach and influence those segments. Finally we measure results and they go back into the database to help form new segments, more refined approaches, and better communications programs.

With this concept in mind, we propose the following types of measures.

Expanded Responses

This measure would include various ways of communicating to the marketer that a message has been received and, most importantly, acted upon. Our approach is based on the idea that every piece of communication should have some form of response that comes back to the marketer; the feedback could be a simple measure of the number of responses generated by various types of integrated marketing coummunications programs. For example, a solicitation might be a prominent 800 number on a package asking the consumer to call for a brochure or more information, or it might be a coupon in the regular newspaper advertisement with an offer to add the consumer's name to a mailing list. A solicitation also could be the listing of special offers by retailers who stock or carry a product. The goal of expanded response is simply to increase the response of current or existing communications programs or techniques that will be used on a regular basis. The goal here is to provide more information or communication that the consumer would like to have or needs to generate the development of some sort of relationship between the buyer and the seller.

Network Change

All consumers have formed some sort of mental network about brands, products, and companies, and how these all fit together.

These associations and affiliations determine the purchasing protocol of consumers. Brand or product networks are formed by all the types of communications that occur over time and from widely varying sources. Thus while these networks are dynamic, they can be measured, particularly over time. Therefore another measure of the impact of an integrated marketing communications program would be changes in brand networks. The closer the brand is tied to the category, the more likely it is that brand loyalty exists. One of the important measures of communications effect is movement in the brand network. We argue that a consumer who changes his or her brand network as a result of an IMC program has demonstrated a behavioral change that is just as important long-term as a purchasing decision.

Contact Measures

Contact measures are those activities in which the consumer initiates contact with the manufacturer as a result of the integrated marketing communications program. An example is a customer or prospect who picks up a folder at a product display, writes or calls for more information, asks friends or neighbors about the marketer's product, or actively accesses information the marketer makes available. These behaviors signify that the consumer has increasing interest in the product or service.

Commitment Measures

While not a transaction, a commitment will likely result some time later in a favorable behavior toward a brand. A commitment includes a wide variety of consumer behaviors, any of which can signify future intentions. Examples include actions such as requesting to be put on a mailing list, filling out an application blank, or attending a demonstration meeting or information session. A commitment also can be explained by having purchased in the past or being a past owner of the product or service. We contend that consumers who have used or purchased the product or service in the past are the ones most likely to do so again if properly motivated with an IMC program.

Purchasers

These are active customers who have purchased the product on a continuing basis. We make no distinction at this point about the volume of the product or service that these customers use. We are interested only in measurable present purchasing activities. From these activitites, we can develop relationships that we hope will build usage and satisfaction over time.

Obviously, these classifications will not fit every company or organization. They are intended only to illustrate the concept of what to measure in an integrated marketing communications program. Each organization must construct the measurement grid or continuum that works best for their product or service and their market. It should be clear, however, that the IMC concept is based on a relationship-building continuum along which customers and prospects move as their relationship with the marketing organization develops. And it should be clear also that in our approach to IMC some type of measurable behavior must occur. We will continue to repeat this concept for we believe it is the key to any type of success in IMC.

8

How to Measure Consumer Responses: Establishing Effective Two-Way Communication

▼

Plan in Advance

The first step in measuring consumer responses to integrated marketing communications is simple: plan for measurement in advance. When the IMC program is planned, two steps should be taken: response devices either should be built into the communications activities or the communications programs should be designed to encourage a measurable response from the consumer. This often means making a change in the way a marketer thinks about the communications program. It means moving from traditional one-way communication to two-way communication. It means that the marketer is interested in more than just sending out messages. Instead, the marketer wants to receive a response that will dictate the type and manner to be used in the next round of communication.

Each Contact Must Be a Communication Device

As we have stressed throughout this text, each contact the consumer has with the marketer's product or service is a form of communication. The real challenge for the IMC manager/planner is to know what contact messages are being made. Then he or she must devise ways to integrate these messages into seamless streams of communication that build and enhance the consumer's feelings, attitudes, and behavior toward the brand. With our expanded concept of communication, it is vital that the marketer have a thorough understanding of the types of contacts being made with consumers. This likely will require much more market monitoring than traditionally has been done. It means that marketers must look not just at what they and their competitors are saying to consumers about the brand, but that they know what others such as consumer groups, retailers, the media, and even other consumers are saying about the category and the brand. Only by understanding all the brand and product contacts consumers have can a true integrated marketing commuications program be planned and implemented.

Soliciting Responses

A critical issue in integrated marketing communications programs is the need for a two-way flow of information. The marketer must actively solicit responses from the consumer. The marketer also must make the consumer know that he or she really wants those responses and will use them to enhance the relationship. Thus customer services, complaints, questions, and inquiries must take top priority in the marketing organization of the future. Every response from the consumer must be captured, stored, and analyzed. These tell a marketer what the consumer really thinks and feels about the brand and set the basis for all future IMC programs.

Responses to the Database

To practice integrated marketing communications, the marketer has already committed to a database. The database is the key to all integrated marketing communications. A critical task is for the marketer to find easy and inexpensive ways to capture, store, and attach the consumer responses to the proper person or group in the database. This generally means that some type of on-line access and input system must be set up. Marketing and communications people must be able to continuously update, change, and enhance the information contained in the files on a real-time basis. The best examples of capture-enhance-update systems today are those used by catalog marketers such as Land's End, Spiegel, and L.L. Bean; or by credit card organizations such as American Express, Visa, and Discover. While some may argue that an on-line capability can be an enormous expense, the expense is not prohibitive when compared to the cost of wasted advertising campaigns. Today, the cost of a database is simply one of the expenses of doing business in the new marketplace.

Respond and Build Flow

The final part of the consumer response measurement process is the analysis of the incoming information, the consumer responses, and the enhanced database. Simply capturing and storing consumer information is of little value. Systems must be devised that analyze consumer responses for trends, changes, concerns, and plaudits so that there will be much more emphasis on customer and database modeling than there has been in the past. This new process also signals a major change in how marketers gather and analyze data. Rather than continuous aggregation to the largest common denominator, the marketer will likely want to dissect masses of currently aggregated data into pieces and parts which can be studied and analyzed. New statistical analysis procedures will be needed to handle the massive databases on which some marketers such as Sears, Philip Morris, and others currently depend. The goal will be to separate and then re-aggregate population segments into groups that make up the communications segments for IMC programs.

The analysis procedure will be one of the most important parts of the IMC program. Only by knowing and understanding what all the consumer responses mean can the integrated marketing communications program be properly planned and effectively implemented. The database analysis area is the least developed portion of the IMC evaluation process, but it is critical to success.

After considering the processes of soliciting and evaluating responses, we now look at how responses can be measured. We start by measuring consumer brand networks.

How to Measure Changes in the Brand Network

Because of the traditional difficulty in measuring in-market behavior of consumers, marketing organizations have developed and used a number of surrogate approaches. Many of these measures are based on measuring consumer attitudes, opinions, and perceptions toward products and services and on self-reported expectations of future purchasing behavior. While some of these measures have proven to be valid, there have been major difficulties in relating these mental measures to what consumers actually do or to how they perform in the marketplace. The major problem is that most consumers, even if they have strong opinions of products and services, are influenced by market factors such as price, availability, and past experience. Typically, they do not include these influences when they state what they intend to do. As a result, most marketers have chosen to measure attitudes, opinions, and perceptions of the marketing communications messages, and to infer purchase behavior. Marketers traditionally have avoided trying to measure actual purchase behavior.

In today's marketplace, we have fairly accurate measures of actual consumer purchase behavior. These come from purchase data available through scanners, from purchases made directly from the manufacturer, through the increased use of warranties and service policies, and from unobtrusive measures such as credit card purchases. Where it once was almost impossible to measure individual purchasing behavior, it is increasingly commonplace to do so. We can now move to measuring a new level of consumer behavior; that is, we can measure behavior first and then use consumer attitudes, opinions, and perceptions to explain the behavior, rather than the other way around. In this section, we discuss some of the ways that consumers' brand networks can be measured and understood.

Moving toward the Center of the Network

In Chapter 3, we illustrated the concept of the brand network, of how consumers mentally store ideas about products, services, and brands. We suggested that consumers' thinking is organized in a hierarchy of network structures. Further, we said that the way brands are organized and stored in the mind is critical to understanding how and under what circumstances consumers will purchase certain brands and products and most likely reject others. If we adapt that concept of a network hierarchy to a series of concentric circles, the techniques of measurement will be understood more easily. In Exhibit 8-1, we have rearranged the illustration from Exhibit 3-2 in a multi-dimensional space.

▼ *Exhibit 8-1*

Hypothetical Beverage Hierarchy

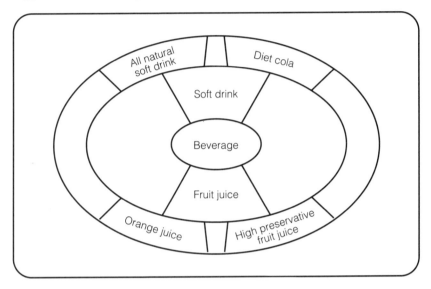

As you can see, the superordinate level is now in the center. The next ring is the basic level and the final ring is the subordinate level. Earlier, we argued that the closer the brand can place itself to the superordinate or basic level, the more likely the person is to buy that brand. If, indeed, the product replaces the category at the basic level, it is likely that the person will buy only that brand and will not even consider other brands no matter what inducement or messages he or she is given.

To understand how brand networks are organized, we must be able to measure the network. Two research approaches are appropriate: laddering and multidimensional scaling.

Laddering

The research technique called laddering helps researchers understand the various hierarchical category, product, and brand levels that generally exist in a consumer's mind. The technique consists of a researcher, generally in a one-on-one situation, conducting an in-depth interview with a typical consumer. The research objective is to get beyond the superficial reasons people normally use to explain their behavior and to reach the real reasons people act and react as they do. This is done through a series of questions that probe ever deeper into a person's mental network. An example will help explain the process and approach.

John Howard, an advertising researcher, has suggested that the total meaning of a brand, its semantic structure, refers to a hierarchy of categories into which a brand is placed by a consumer. This hierarchical classification structure consists basically of attitudes and beliefs about a product, the choice criteria upon which evaluation is based and the values specific to the consumer that affect the relative importance of the respective choice criteria.

Building on Howard's work, Gutman and Reynolds used a means-end chain concept to show how consumers group products differentially at the different levels of abstraction. This was accomplished by a laddering method (consisting of in-depth probing as to the reasons a respondent identifies a concept as being important), which moves consumers to higher levels of abstraction in order to obtain responses closer to the "end," or values level. In theory, it is this higher values level that governs perception and ultimately, product evaluation.

The laddering procedure elicits a connected set or chain of interrelated descriptive elements. (See Exhibit 8-2.) The

▼ **Exhibit 8-2**

The Concept and Process of Laddering

Source: Patricia Cafferata and Alice Tybout, *Cognitive and Affective Response to Advertising* (Lexington, Mass: Lexington Books, 1989), 374–376.

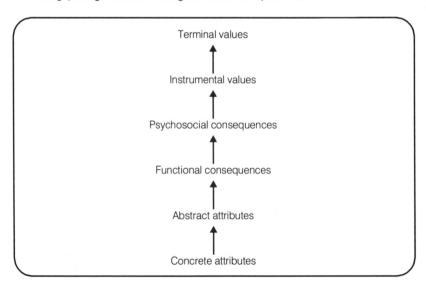

connections among these elements are the basis of associated meaning in the consumer's mind and thus are assumed to be of key importance to understanding choice behavior. In their original laddering study, Gutman and Reynolds found the largest chain of elements (ranging from an attribute to a value) obtained from the individual respondent was considered to be the most relevant and can thus be used for further analysis. Using one element of the chain at a time as a basis for distinction, products can be sorted into groups such that each group forms a set of similar products. As would be expected, a qualitative summary of the resulting data reveals that (1) initial levels of distinction are primarily concerned with contents or physical aspects of products, and (2) subsequent levels move to more abstract, personal distinctions representative of values.

Through this "laddering" approach, we can start to understand how the mental networks of consumers are constructed and how various concepts are connected. The ideal solution to this approach is to illustrate these networks graphically so that they can be studied and perhaps modeled.

Multidimensional Scaling

An alternative method to laddering relies on a sophisticated statistical approach called multidimensional scaling or MDS. MDS measures consist of a series of questions about various product, brand, or category attributes that are to be measured. Generally, this is done through some sort of scaled measure approach. Then, using a computer routine, these concepts are related to each other in the form of a multidimensional map that illustrates the relationships.

The perceptual map generated by *multidimensional scaling* is illustrated in Exhibit 8-3. In this technique, consumers are asked to rate each pair of products in terms of their degree of similarity using a scale such as that in (B). These similarity judgments are then analyzed by statistical programs that determine the relative closeness of the brands from the perspective of the target market customers as a whole. Because traditional multidimensional scaling approaches map only the similarity judgments, the reasons why some pairs of brands are more similar than other pairs must be inferred. So, the axis in (A) will normally have to be labeled based on the researcher's judgment.

▼   **Exhibit 8-3**

An Example of MDS Mapping

Source: Adapted from Joseph P. Guiltinau and Gordon W. Paul, *Marketing Management, Strategies and Programs*, 4th ed. (New York: Prentice-Hall, 1991), 83–84.

(A)

•
Almost Home
Duncan Hines
•

Grandma's
•

•
Soft Batch

•
Chippy Chews

A perceptual map of the moist and chewy cookie market using multidimensional scaling.

(B)	Very similar				Very different
Grandma's/Duncan Hines	1	2	3	4	5
Grandma's/Almost Home	—	—	—	—	—
Grandma's/Soft Batch	—	—	—	—	—
Grandma's/Chippy Chews	—	—	—	—	—
Duncan Hines/Almost Home	—	—	—	—	—
.					
.					
.					
Soft Batch/Chippy Chews	—	—	—	—	—

The advantage of MDS is that the system is able to relate concepts, opinions, attitudes, and even perceptions in several different ways. Often, MDS maps reveal more than simple two-dimensional charts about how consumers store ideas and notions.

No matter what the research technique, the goal of brand network research is to understand how consumers have constructed brand networks in their heads. By knowing this, the IMC manager can start to understand why good customers have certain networks and poor customers often have totally different networks. With this information, the IMC manager can start to define the best possible network for building brand loyalty. By knowing that certain behaviors are the result of specific attitudes, opinions, and beliefs put together in certain ways, the marketer could then start to design communications programs that would influence these networks. This, of course, is the objective of all IMC programs.

Pre-Post Tests

The best way to measure changes in or impacts on a consumer's mental networks about brands is through some type of pre-post measurement. This means that the marketer measures the mental network of the consumer prior to developing any type of marketing communications effort. The measurement forms the base line for a customer or group.

With an understanding how networks of good customers are organized, the marketer can develop messages or contacts that would influence the consumer to adjust his or her networks to resemble those of good customers. Once these messages have been delivered, the marketer would conduct a follow-up or post-test. This research would measure the success of the marketing communications program in getting consumers to change their networks. The marketer could then compare the original network map with the one that emerges following the IMC program. This comparison would tell whether or not the program was successful.

Although we have suggested that messages alone can constitute the IMC program, it is quite possible that the marketer also might include consumer actions. These behavioral messages then would result in the desired brand, product, or category network shifts. This, of course, depends to a great extent on the understanding of the IMC manager and the information available in the customer database.

Measurement of the consumer network is only one of the measures possible in IMC. We next discuss how to measure contacts.

How to Measure Contacts

Contacts will likely be a new term for many advertising and promotion people, particularly in the way it is used in IMC. We define a contact as any information-bearing experience that a customer or prospect has with the brand, the product category, or the market that relates to the marketer's product or service. With this approach there are hundreds if not thousands of ways in which a person can come in contact with a brand. For example, a contact can include friends' and neighbors' comments, packaging, newspaper, magazine, and television information, ways the customer or prospect is treated in the retail store, where the product is shelved in the store, and the type of signage that appears in retail establishments. And the contacts do not stop with the purchase. Contacts also consist of what friends, relatives, and bosses say about a person who is using the product. Contacts include the type of customer service given with returns or inquiries, or even the types of letters the company writes to resolve problems or to solicit additional business. All of these are customer contacts with the brand. These bits and pieces of information, experiences, and relationships, created over time, influence the potential relationship among the customer, the brand, and the marketer.

Obviously, the marketing organization has control over some consumer contacts and little or no control over many of the others. The question here is how to inventory, measure, or identify all the contact points the customer has with the brand or product. Then the challenge is to determine which contacts are most important, which really create changes in the consumer's brand network or influence product purchase or usage behavior. We examine first the idea of a contact inventory.

Contact Inventories

All customers and prospects have an inventory of contacts with the brand or product. For example, most people can remember a few salient points in their lives that led them to either begin or to continue using the brands they now purchase routinely. For example, with toothpaste, one may remember what Mom bought and said we should use. With automobiles, a consumer may have had a number of experiences with various brands over a period of time. With stock brokers there may have been advice from relatives or close friends. In any case, most people probably can identify some contacts that led them to start using their present brands. Often, when consumers discuss these brand contacts, there is little or no mention of advertising, promotion, or other forms of commercial, persuasive communication. Most of us don't like to confess that we have been influenced in that way. Thus a manager's first step is to conduct a customer inventory of major contacts that influenced brand or product purchase.

With this inventory, the IMC manager can start to identify the major contact points that relatively large numbers of people associate with the brand or product. A common way to do this is through a series of focus group sessions. Then survey research can be used to help identify those contacts that most people remember or that are cited by various consumer groups such as users, non-users, loyal buyers, and switch buyers. The goal is to identify the contact points that customers use to explain their present behavior. This is the base of information that must be identified and categorized before an effective IMC program can be developed. Identification is generally the first step in the behavioral segmentation process that was discussed in Chapter 5.

Contact Paths

Once the base line of contacts is established, the next step is to understand what contacts consumers have with the brand on the way to making a purchasing decision. Generally, this requires the consumer to walk through the buying process for a product or service. For example, an individual could be asked to go through his or her process of purchasing a pound of coffee. The person would be asked to think about all the contacts he or she has had with the product and product category as he or she has gone about making the purchase. An example of this type of contact mapping is illustrated in Exhibit 8-4 on the next four pages.

▼   *Exhibit 8-4*

IBM Contact Maps

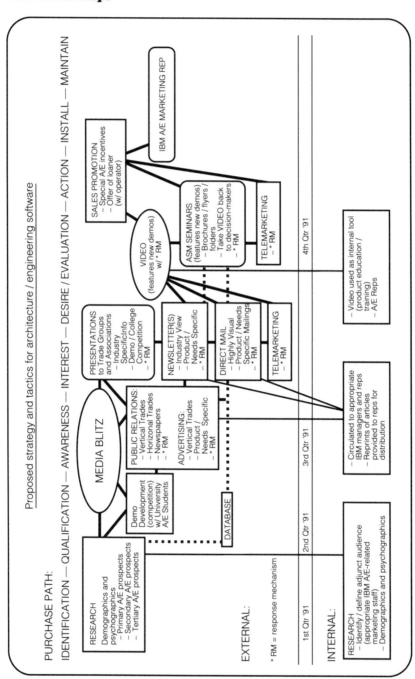

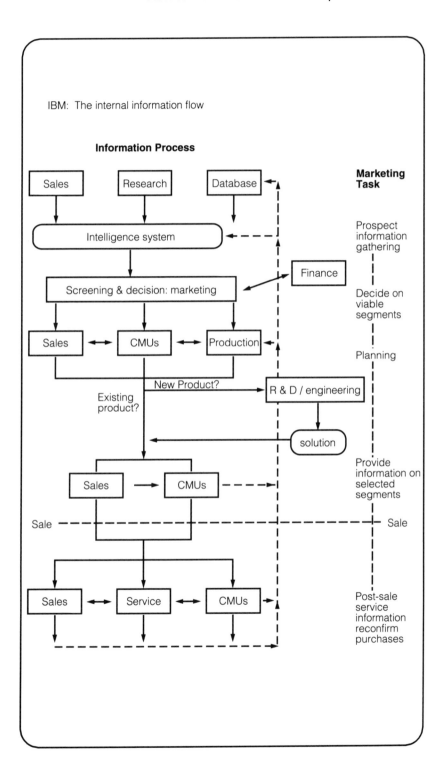

IBM: The internal information flow

Exhibit 8-4 continued

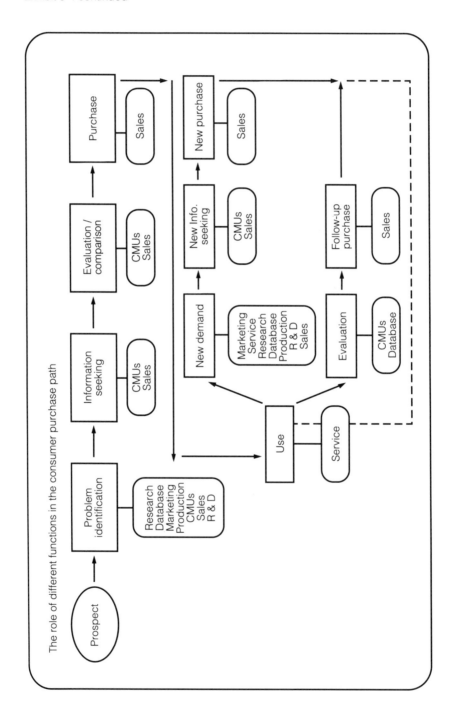

The role of different functions in the consumer purchase path

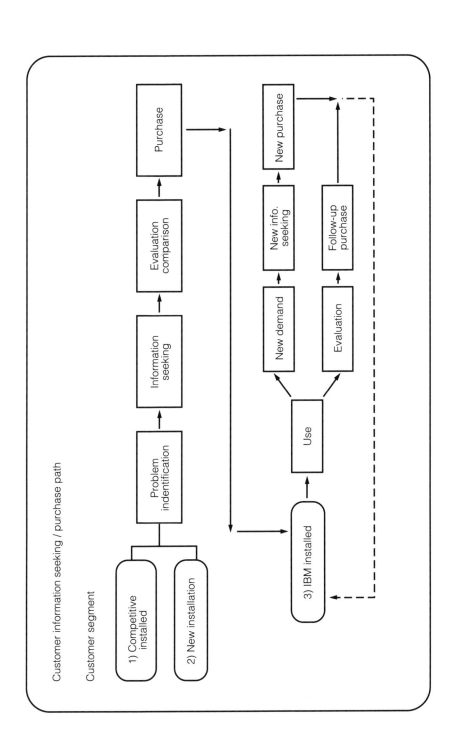

As you can see, the consumer can have a wide variety of contacts with the brand and the category before making a purchase. The concern of the IMC manager is twofold:

> **1** to identify those points along the contact path that seem to be the most critical in the purchase decision process; and
>
> **2** to identify the points in the path at which the prospect can be reached with a persuasive brand message.

By knowing these critical points, the IMC manager can develop information contacts that can be used to influence the customer or prospect. In addition, this contact path approach sets up a measurement system. When the contact points are identified, the manager can determine whether or not the prospect was reached with the integrated marketing communications message.

Tracking Studies

The most common approach to developing a measurement of contacts is through some form of tracking study. A tracking study is a series of measurements over time of the messages that are delivered to the customer or prospect and of the changes in behavior that result due to those messages. For example, advertising managers traditionally have tried to track the impact of their media-delivered messages by means of pre-post tests in some sort of experimental situation. This same pre-post approach could be used to measure customer contacts. The system would have to be broadened considerably, however, for IMC to include both paid and non-paid media plus marketplace contacts and competitive messages as well.

The DDB Needham advertising agency has develop an approach that they call "media mapping." The approach offers some potential in this area. The DDB Needham system asks groups of consumers to identify their media exposures during a certain period of time. For example, a person wakes up in the morning to a clock radio. The person reads the newspaper on the way to work, is exposed to train or bus posters along the way and sees outdoor advertising near his or her office. He or she glances through a magazine at a newsstand, watches television that evening, and so on. By identifying the media to which consumers were exposed and learning what advertising or messages were contained in those media during that time, DDB Needham people can make assumptions about when the media contacts were made with the consumer.

Expanding the Tracking Study

While a tracking system might work for paid, controllable messages that the marketer might initiate, it fails to take into account the wide variety of uncontrolled or uncontrollable messages that a consumer receives about the brand in his or her daily life. To accommodate uncontrollable factors, the IMC marketer must expand his or her view of communications to include these other, often more important contacts.

While no recognized system currently exists for this type of extended consumer communication contact, there are concepts and approaches that can be used. For example, today Lexis/Nexis captures, capsulizes, and categorizes information contained in a wide variety of consumer and trade publications. A review of the stored data in these systems, combined with some type of media map from the consumer, can help identify any articles, stories, and messages that might have reached the customer or prospect. Through content analysis, fairly broad categorical elements can be identified with computer searches of current or historical editorial material. A review of the material from traditional clipping services also can provide this type of information. It is likely that, in the not-too-distant future, computer searches of yesterday's major media will not only be possible but practical as well. So while at present the IMC manager is somewhat limited in what can be identified and measured outside of self-reported information, the time is not far distant when a more accurate consumer inventory will be possible.

Measuring Known Contacts

As we mentioned earlier, the critical ingredients in IMC are encouraging responses and the development of a two-way form of communication between the buyer and the seller. The IMC marketer must, at every occasion, encourage the customer or prospect to provide some type of feedback about the product, the service received, or the satisfaction level. This is particularly important in the contact path.

One of the easiest ways to measure contacts is through known experiences that the consumer has had with the product. For example, the IMC marketer must solicit information about the purchaser or user's contact with the product. There must be built-in response devices that encourage the consumer to let the marketer know about his or her experience. These devices can be mail-back cards, toll-free telephone numbers, warranty cards, etc. However, the concept of these reply devices must be expanded. The warranty card no longer can be just a record of purchase; it must encourage the purchaser to tell the marketer what he or she liked about the product and what contact path the person took to the purchase. The IMC marketer must constantly seek all forms of information about customer and prospect contacts with the brand, the product, and the organization.

Capturing Responses

Perhaps the most critical part of the contact path approach is capturing and recording the contact responses provided by the consumer. Whenever possible, the incoming information about customer contacts must be stored and analyzed. Through customer modeling, such as the use of scoring models currently employed by catalog marketers, the IMC marketer can re-aggregate customer groups based on their contact paths or their use of contact information. While each organization will need to develop its own system for contact mapping and customer aggregation, the IMC marketer should plan in advance for the gathering and use of this information in the evaluation process.

How to Measure Consumer Commitment

So far, the behavioral measures that we have discussed have been those in which the consumers have had to make a mental change or adaptation to what they previously had stored. While mental changes are important, the goal of IMC is to move as close as possible to the actual purchase behavior of the consumer.

The next logical step in measuring behavior is to develop a measure of the purchasing commitment of the persons to whom our IMC programs have been directed. We might think of this commitment process as one in which the targeted person "holds up his hand" to signify interest. In other words, the prospect has committed to some type of relationship with the marketer although the commitment may not yet have resulted in a purchase.

To turn those consumer commitments into actual sales, the marketer must understand what those commitments mean, how they might be measured and how IMC programs might be developed which, with proper cultivation, might blossom into sales and long-term relationships.

What is a Commitment?

For our purposes, we define a consumer commitment as an external demonstration of interest in either the marketer's brand or in the generic or a related category. This commitment can be a physical interest in the brand, such as an inquiry. It may also be implied as a result of some other behavior, such as the purchase of a related product or one that might signify interest in the brand's category. The most obvious example of a commitment would be the receipt of a letter or coupon requesting more information after a person sees some type of marketing communication for the brand. An alternative might be a call to an 800 number or even a visit to the retailer who carries the brand. While a sale may not have necessarily taken place, if the marketer has the proper measurement systems in place, he or she knows of this interest and that a commitment has been made. Based on this, the marketer can develop with the prospect an IMC program that will turn the initial commitment into a sale.

A perhaps less obvious example of a commitment might be the action taken by a woman who buys a new set of golf clubs. Our marketer does not sell golf clubs but he does sell golf clothing. By purchasing golf clubs, the lady has identified herself as being interested in golf. She has made a commitment. She has "held up her hand." This makes her a much better prospect than another woman of the same age bracket or income level or even one who has a husband who plays golf. It is this indication of interest in the product or service that the marketer needs to capture and measure, for people who give such indications are generally the best prospects for an integrated marketing communications program.

The marketer can measure consumer commitments through the use of either external or internal approaches. Both are discussed in the following sections.

External Measures

Most of the external measures of consumer commitment come from various forms of market research. There are basically three types of market research: syndicated studies, data overlays, and affiliations.

Syndicated studies are conducted by research suppliers who gather information from a consumer sample. The research organization then sells the results, generally in some aggregated form, to interested marketers. For example, the well-known Simmons and MRI data are syndicated studies. A research organization conducts the study and any interested company can purchase the information for their own uses. There are many other types of consumer information resources. Data often is gathered by research organizations, but trade associations, the media, and consumer groups also conduct these types of studies. The key questions for the IMC manager to ask are how the data was gathered, for what purpose it was gathered, and whether it is accurate and current.

Data overlays are files of information that have been gathered by research or other organizations. These files can be overlaid, or appended to the marketer's customer or prospect file through a computer routine. For example, if an auto marketer were interested in determining how many new car prospects lived in a certain community, this could be done by (a) constructing a file of all present customer households in the community, (b) overlaying the R. L. Polk file over that list (the Polk file would hold the automobile registration information that has been obtained from the state for each automobile owned by each household), and (c) setting an arbitrary age for the automobile, say older than five years. The marketer then could request that only those households having a five-year-old or older automobile be identified. With this overlay approach, the marketer can develop a list of consumers in the community with automobiles five years old or older. In the broadest sense, ownership would be a consumer commitment. At some point the consumer most likely will buy another car. By making a commitment to own an automobile, the consumer also may have made a commitment to purchase another car in the future. At the least, the consumer certainly has committed to buy the products and services necessary for the car's upkeep in the meantime.

Affiliations are the final way in which commitment can be identified. A person who belongs to a social, political, religious, or fraternal organization has signified a commitment of some type to that group. By measuring this relationship, the marketer may be able to make assumptions about how these commitments relate to his or her product or service. The affiliation approach can also be used in a number of ways. For example, subscribing to a magazine, becoming a member of a local club, or subscribing to cultural events such as operas, dance programs, and theater performances indicate a person's commitment to the organization. Even knowledge of charitable organization membership or donations can be helpful to some marketers.

An excellent example of the affiliation concept is illustrated by membership in the American Association of Retired Persons (AARP), a consumer group of persons over the age of 50. This group provides a number of services to its members. Membership in AARP identifies a person's interests and likely purchase decisions. By purchasing AARP's membership list and checking it against the database of existing customers or prospects, the marketer can develop a commitment measure for a key group of people.

No matter what external measure is used, the real key to benefiting from a commitment measure is the relationship between the marketer's products and the external measure being used. There must be a strong, proven correlation for commitment to be of much value. The correlation generally can be found as a result of extensive work with the marketer's own database. In researching his own ownership, membership, or customer file, the marketer may learn that most individuals in his database are members of a certain social club, own a specific make of automobile, or have a dog as a pet. These factors then can be used to help develop more effective IMC programs. The ability to use "inferential marketing" is really one of the great strengths of IMC marketing.

Internal Measures

In sophisticated organizations that are practicing IMC, the marketer would first measure his or her own database to determine what type of commitment measures could be found. We will assume here that, for the most part, many marketers do not yet have a substantial customer database. Therefore, we will approach the internal measure portion of this section from a zero base; that is, we assume the marketer is interested in identifying or generating commitments from customers or prospects but has little actual data.

Solicit Response

The first step in the IMC process is to generate response. To accomplish this the marketer must solicit response. All communications programs have two things in common, they have a response device built into them and they encourage customers, prospects, casual users, and even those considered to be non-prospects to communicate back to the marketer in some way. While direct marketers will find this concept very basic, those in advertising, public relations, or even sales promotion may consider it somewhat unique. For marketers who have been using these tools separately, considerable effort may be required to develop effective IMC programs that solicit effective responses.

Responses can be generated from communications programs in a number of ways. The most common are the inclusion of a response coupon, the provision of a toll-free 800 number, or the inclusion of a low-toll 900 number. All advertisements should have a coupon or other device by which a prospect can request more information. Packages should have an 800 number. Press and news releases should state how more information can be obtained. Directions included with the product should have addresses and phone numbers. In short, every piece of material, every contact that the consumer or prospect has with the brand should include some type of feedback or response provision. Only in this way can the database be built and only in this way can IMC be practiced.

Next Steps in Commitment Measurement and Control

Obviously, if responses are sought from consumers, they should be used. If the prospects raise their hands, they expect some response from the marketer. It is in this area of handling responses and inquiries that many marketing organizations destroy the value of their communications program. When the customer signifies a commitment in the form of a response, an inquiry, a request for more information, or a store or dealer visit, it is critical that the marketer follow up quickly and effectively. Inquiries should be treated as quickly as complaints. Requests for information must be sent in the fastest possible way. A store visit must be acknowledged and followed up. In short, once the prospect has signified an interest, or "raised a hand," every communication tool should be used to turn that prospect into a customer.

As before, the critical element is the marketer's database. Only through the use of an extensive, sophisticated database designed to provide IMC support is this possible. The marketer must make a major commitment to the IMC program because IMC is likely to fail if the systems have not been developed to support new programs. While the construction and design of computer databases are beyond the scope of this text, it is clear that specific IMC databases are needed, rather than databases that are attached to an accounting or bookkeeping system.

The final step in the IMC development process is the development of customer and prospect models based on the commitment responses that have been generated and stored in the database. The modeling often can be done simply by tracking various groups of persons who have made commitments and eventually turned into customers. This approach would provide the first step in understanding the flow of these groups into the customer base. For example, a traditional lead-tracking system could be used in this process. Such a system is simple to set up if the data is captured and then related back to the prospect over time. Time series analysis can then be used to understand any changes. Information generated by the analysis will generally provide clues as to how prospects move into the customer base. From this, modeling can be done. The critical elements in such a system are the types of marketing communications programs that were used, the response rates, and the results of the various efforts. Through these efforts one can start to understand the impact of the individual communications efforts and the effects of these elements when used in combination.

We now turn to the measurement of actual purchases.

How to Measure Customer Purchases

Although we have emphasized the importance of consumer and customer behavior and the value of capturing and storing information about such behavior in a database, actually measuring purchases is probably the most important step in developing an effective integrated marketing communications program. Unfortunately, except among direct marketers, the skill of capturing purchase data is not well developed, particularly in those organizations that market through several levels of retail distribution. Yet gathering such information is critical for the future of IMC. In this section we discuss the needs and capabilities required of those organizations that are able to measure purchases directly, those that can measure indirectly, and those that must try to identify customers in complex distribution channels.

Direct Measures

While many direct marketers pride themselves on being involved in database marketing, many use the term quite loosely. In effect, while they may sell direct, they use direct marketing techniques and systems only to mass market to relatively unknown groups of people. This is particularly true for those direct marketers who use the broadcast media or make mass mailings to outside lists.

Real database marketing, the type necessary for integrated marketing communications programs, requires the identification of customers by name, address, perhaps some demographics, and psychographics if they are appropriate. The most critical element to identify is customer purchase history. Only by having this information can a marketer really start to practice two-way or relationship marketing. For the most part, this type of information presently is gathered by measuring direct purchases and supplementing this measurement with credit or other personal information. Such information commonly is gathered through some type of credit application or through the use of a credit rating organization.

To use this approach, the marketer must record every purchase and every item purchased by the customer. Generally, this is done electronically and is gathered at the household level.

By capturing purchase information, the marketer can identify which parts of his or her communications program worked and which didn't. Catalog and some direct mail organizations do this now. They code each communication and then tie the actual purchase response back to the communication unit. For example, Land's End codes each catalog it mails to a customer. When the customer orders, the order clerk asks for the code numbers on the catalog. In this way, Land's End knows which catalogs worked and can start to determine why they worked. This is the type of feedback that is critical in the development of an IMC program.

By knowing actual purchase data and the communication form that generated it, direct marketers can start to estimate which communications techniques worked well and which didn't. At the same time, they can start to estimate the type of response they might get from future communications efforts. This understanding of the impact of each individual communication element is critical in understanding how the elements work in combination. More on this later.

Indirect Purchase Measures

Unfortunately, not all marketers have the detailed purchase information that direct selling provides—the purchase history and the ability to relate a communication technique directly back to the individual customer or household. Most organizations that sell through various forms of wholesalers, dealers, or distributors lack this information. In these cases, the marketer knows only a limited amount about the customer base. Generally, the marketer knows only the geographic area where the dealer is located, some general demographic information about the customer base, and something about income levels. Most of this information is aggregated in some way so that it is difficult to understand what is happening to individual customers. In these situations, the marketer must rely on various indirect forms of measurement to build the required database.

One of the best methods of learning about a customer base served through retail channels is through service or warranty cards. A warranty is given with many products in the form of a card packed with the product. The person who purchases the product completes the card and mails it back to the manufacturer. On this card, the marketer commonly asks a series of questions about the purchase of the product such as (a) in what type of store was the product purchased, (b) the reason for the purchase, and (c) whether the product was a new addition or a replacement. Some marketers have used this technique to gather information about areas beyond the specific product. For example, questions about ownership of associated products might be asked. A ski manufacturer might ask about camera ownership or a bicycle manufacturer might want to know about other outdoor sports or hobbies in which the purchaser is involved. In each case, the goal is to build a database with as much information as possible to allow the marketer to identify the types of customers they have. The same approach can be used with service calls, service programs, product attachments, and add-ons. In this way, the company can begin to build a database of known customers.

While the return level of warranty or service cards in many product categories is fairly low compared with the number of items sold, this approach is one way to build a minimal-level customer database that can be used in developing IMC programs.

Measuring Purchases through Complex Channels

Perhaps the most difficult purchase measurement is tracking the sale of fast-moving, low-cost consumable products. These include such things as foods, beverages, beer and wine, and clothing. For each of these product categories, there may be numerous retail outlets. The customer often uses up these products fairly quickly and repurchases at a number of different locations. While the problems of purchase measurement may be somewhat different for apparel than for beverages, we will use the food category as an example since it is generally the most advanced in terms of trying to build customer databases. Two approaches commonly are used.

Measurement of the marketer's own promotional activities is the easiest way to capture at least names and addresses of customers and prospects. Information can be requested through various forms of promotional activities such as contests, sweepstakes, and premium orders. While there is no verifiable evidence of purchase involved in these types of promotional activities (although some marketers do request that the consumer send in proofs of purchase), there is at least some evidence of commitment to the product.

The critical elements in using promotional material to identify and classify prospects and customers are:

1   the needed information for the database must be identified and included with the promotional piece;

2   the response must be coded in some way so that it can be traced back to the respondent;

3   there must be provision for the capture and recording of the names and communication approaches used based on the returns.

Many organizations such as the Quaker Oats Co., Philip Morris, and Kraft General Foods have built substantial databases using these types of information gathering.

Purchase of syndicated data such as scanner panel or diary information is the second major method of capturing actual purchase behavior data from individual consumers. Today, many retail and some research organizations are capturing actual individual household level purchase data through various forms of panels and frequent purchaser programs. The programs are quite simple in concept but quite complex in application.

Retailers or research organizations solicit consumers to join a shopper panel. Generally, these programs are designed to reward the shoppers with price discounts, prizes, and awards for participation. The consumer is given an encoded card which is then used each time he or she shops. The identification code on the card is read by a computer. The consumer purchases are identified through the Universal Product Code (UPC) found on most packaged consumer products. The customer code–product purchase connection is then made electronically and stored in a database.

Food and drug stores, mass merchandisers, and other types of retailers often make this customer purchase information available to their marketer suppliers. In this way the marketer can identify which households are purchasing his or her products, with what frequency, and at what price. Thus customer databases for products that are widely used and purchased rather frequently can be developed. If the data is available over time, the marketer can start to understand the various purchasing strategies that the consumer households use in the marketplace. In addition, it is possible to identify which parts of the marketing communications program were the most effective in terms of motivating customers to purchase. The major advantage of this type of customer data is that it describes individual households. Thus the marketer can start to understand how each household responds to each form of marketing communications. In addition, scanner data allows the marketer to do considerable testing of marketing techniques. For example, tests can be set up in which several communications offers, perhaps using differing media forms, can be tested against each other. In addition, the marketer can learn what the impact of marketing communications programs are over time. The marketer also can see the impact of a combination of communications techniques. This combination is perhaps the most interesting output that scanner panels provide today.

In the future, as we move more and more to electronic funds transfers, debit systems, and a "cashless" society, electronic data capture will be more and more important to marketers. It will enable them to understand and evaluate the impact of various forms of marketing communications that have been integrated into an overall program.

The most difficult issue in using scanner or other types of electronic marketing information in measuring customer purchases is in decomposing the sales bumps produced by a combination of marketing and communications activities. This process is often carried out through various forms of in-store experiments. One of the largest organizations capable of performing these tests is Information Resources, Inc. (IRI) of Chicago. IRI has constructed a number of test markets across the United States in which consumers have agreed to carry a household identification card and to have their purchases scanned and analyzed. By using various forms of experiments and controlling the marketing activities, IRI has developed some interesting theories about how merchandising and promotion activities act and interact. An example of the type of information that IRI is able to generate is illustrated in Exhibit 8-5 below.

IRI has been able to separate the effects of displays as compared with supermarket features for the three categories shown in Exhibit 8-5. (Note that the information in this illustration has been aggregated for the category and for a four week period. The basic

▼ **Exhibit 8-5**

IRI Scanner Panel Data from POS

Source: "Kitchen Yields Odd Combination but More Sales." *P-O-P Times* (June 1991): 29.

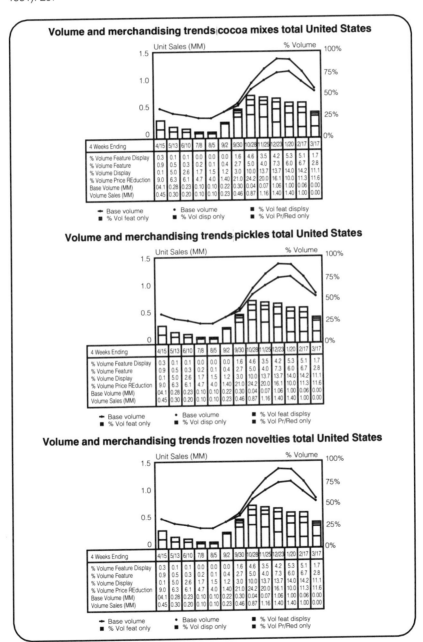

information is based on findings from individual households and the findings have then been aggregated for this example. The power of the technique is evident, however.)

With this look at the measurement of actual purchase data, we can now summarize how various forms of integrated marketing communications programs assist in the development of effective communications programs.

Circular Systems

As should now be evident, what we propose for a successful integrated marketing communications program is a circular system. It works like this:

1   The marketer first develops a database of interested customers or prospects. This can be done in a number of ways, some of which were described in the previous sections.

2   Marketing communications programs are designed and delivered to this interested group through various media and non-media systems; a response is always solicited.

3   The consumer responds in some way, through a purchase, an inquiry for more information, a "holding up of the hand," or a change in the brand network.

4   The marketer takes this information, stores it in some form of database, analyzes the material, and develops a response to the consumer such as another form of communication.

5   The customer or prospect responds again.

What really occurs is almost interpersonal communication although it may be conducted through various media forms and with large numbers of customers and prospects at the same time. This is how integrated marketing communications programs should work. This is the beginning of true "relationship marketing."

The critical ingredients in this sort of IMC system are the database of customers or prospects and the marketer's ability to analyze and re-aggregate these responding consumers into groups such as those with common interests or common needs for information. Messages can be delivered either through the media or directly, whichever is the most effective or efficient method.

The new IMC approach allows marketers to identify, measure, and understand customer responses to the IMC program. It is here that much work needs to the done. Traditionally, marketers have been involved primarily in one-way communication. Therefore, most measurement techniques have been designed to measure message output, receipt, and recall, not responses. While there are some response measurement techniques today such as response cards, 800 numbers, and even scanner data, these devices are still rather crude and unwieldy forms of obtaining and understanding responses from customers and prospects.

Determining the Next Round of Communication

No matter how the response is captured, stored, or analyzed, an important part of an integrated marketing communications program is the determination of the next round of communication to be developed. Here, the outside-in view of planning must dominate. The next campaign must be driven by the response that was received from the consumer. This means that a thorough analysis of the response must be made. In other words, marketers must learn what the consumer said back, what information they wanted and in what form, and so on. Generally this is the most difficult part of the process for marketers. The responses may require a regrouping of the customer and/or prospect base. They may mean that some people must be dropped as prospects. They may even indicate that an internally loved advertising program or sales promotion event must be abandoned. The responses may even show a need for rethinking the whole IMC program. But that is what IMC is all about. It is self-adjusting. It is designed to motivate customers and prospects, not to satisfy the creators of the communications program. In an IMC program, the only constants are change and adaptation. Some marketing communications people have difficulty accepting these facts.

Responding to Customers and Prospects

The response that the marketer makes to the customers and prospects as a result of an integrated marketing communications program is very important. This is where the real relationship starts. To respond successfully, the marketer must truly be interested in developing customers and prospects. Short-term, get-rich-quick approaches simply won't work in IMC. Building trust may be more important than gaining market share; building a relationship may be more vital in the long term than increasing profits in the short term. We do not mean that customers cannot be profitable to the marketing organization. In fact, they may be more profitable as IMC programs build the relationship. But the critical ingredient in an IMC program is the long-term relationship built through various forms of communication. The marketer must truly become customer-driven if he or she is to successfully implement an IMC program.

The Next Stages of Measurement

To this point, we have discussed IMC looking only at available technology and existing marketing communications systems. There is little question that these will change dramatically in the next few years as technology expands and consumers become more accustomed to that technology. Transactional programs and digital delivery and ISDN may well be the systems that will have the greatest impact on IMC programs in the immediate future.

Transactional Programs

The initial efforts of capturing and analyzing customer purchase information through scanner panels and other electronic marketing devices are just that, initial efforts. There is little question that more effective transactional programs will develop rather rapidly. Most likely, these approaches will be tied to the increasing use of electronic funds transfer (EFT) by the financial community. This process will involve all types of retailers, wholesalers, and distributors. As EFT grows, systems will be developed that will instantly process customer transactions in retail settings. The transaction results will give the marketer almost instant knowledge of who is buying, at what location, in what amount, and the price paid. A major question here, of course, is who will capture or own this information. At present, it appears that the retailer or a third party such as a financial institution will own the information. Whatever the case, it is likely that much more customer purchase information will be available. IMC marketers must learn to identify and understand how the communications programs are related to the purchases. This is an area that must be developed quickly as IMC grows.

Digital Delivery and ISDN

On the immediate horizon is the installation of fiber optic cable systems at the household level. These systems will increase enormously the availability of information to each household. Through Integrated Systems Data Networks (ISDN), many forms of electronic communication will arrive in the household through digital delivery. This means that an almost unlimited number of cable television, voice and data systems, telephone, fax, and other systems will enter each home or office. The beauty of this new technology is that it flows both ways, into the home or office and back out of the home or office. Thus consumers not only will be able to receive information from marketers, they will also be able to respond to them on an almost instantaneous, real-time basis. We will have the capability of real two-way communication between the buyer and the seller not only in a local community but around the world.

The new form of electronic data delivery will make it possible for customers and prospects to access the information they need from the marketer *when* they need it. Today, the marketer sends out usable information about a product or service at the marketer's convenience. The marketer almost always initiates the communication. This is communication initiated when the seller wants to sell, not when the buyer wants to buy. With ISDN, the consumer will be able to access information from the seller when needed, at the buyer's convenience. This represents an entirely new way of doing business for most marketers. It means that marketers will need to be responsive to the buyer when the buyer wants to buy. They will need to develop new types of communications programs that make it easy for customers to access information. Marketers will have to make sure that the information the consumer wants is quickly and easily available. Integrated marketing communications will be the minimum level of customer service that a marketer can provide and many organizations will have to go beyond that level to survive.

Integrated marketing communications seems like a difficult process today in our one-way, low-response, marketer-driven communications systems. By early in the twenty-first century, IMC will be so prevalent we will wonder how we ever survived without it.

Barriers to Integration: Overcoming the Stumbling Blocks

▼

To this point, we have described IMC as a solution to many of today's marketing problems. However, acceptance hasn't been as rapid as one would hope. This raises the question: If IMC is such a wonderful concept, why then hasn't every marketing organization embraced the concept and the approach?

Unfortunately, as with many other innovative concepts, there is resistance to change. In most marketing organizations, there are established ways of doing things, solidified positions, turf and budget concerns and, most of all, corporate cultures that have grown to be accepted as the right way to do things. In these types of companies there is no great desire or inclination to change. On the following pages, we will describe some of the most common barriers to IMC. Then we will suggest some solutions that are being used to enable forward-looking organizations to take advantage of the power of IMC in companies and organizations around the world.

Why Doesn't Everyone Buy in Immediately?

The major barrier to IMC is a simple but powerful one: resistance to change within the organization. While all marketing professionals, and particularly marketing communications people, like to think of themselves as innovative, creative, and forward-thinking, most are set in their ways. Most marketing communications managers have found ways to accomplish certain tasks such as campaign development or budgeting or even evaluation. They place great trust in these established approaches. A perfect example is advertising pre-testing. While many marketing communications experts agree that the pre-testing of television commercials is not very predictive nor very enlightening, many marketing communications managers continue to pre-test because they have always pre-tested. Pre-testing may not tell you much, but at least you can say you have pre-tested if the commercial turns out to be a disaster in the marketplace.

There is also a herd mentality in the marketing communications field. If one organization develops a successful technique or new approach, everyone else tends to copy the method whether it is relevant to their organization or not. AT&T's "shaky camera" television commercials of a few years ago spawned a whole generation of imitators. Unfortunately, this same imitative approach is used in everything from organizational structure to media selection. There seems to be strength in numbers in marketing communications, i.e., if lots of organizations are doing something, then it must be right. Thus, because many organizations use functional management structures or the traditional awareness-preference-conviction advertising model these approaches gain a certain legitimacy. That acceptance by the group is difficult to change.

While personal and organizational resistance to change is the major barrier to IMC, there are three basic organizational issues which must be resolved for the concept to work. They are:

1   Marketing planning systems and basic marketing thinking

2   Organizational structures

3   Capabilities and control

We will deal with each of these issues and provide some solutions on the following pages. We start with the most common of the three barriers to IMC, marketing planning systems and basic marketing thinking.

Planning Systems and Marketing Thinking

Most organizations have developed a very structured approach to marketing planning that may or may not be recognized within the organization. This has come about as organizations have increasingly moved toward financial analysis as the critical area of marketing. Originally, marketing was allied with sales. That is, marketing was a more disciplined way of thinking about how to sell the products or services that an organization made or developed. Over the years, however, marketing has increasingly focused on financial analysis, generally dealing with microeconomic approaches such as marginal analysis and forecasting.

As marketing became more financially driven, more and more of the emphasis was turned inward toward the company or the organization rather than outward toward the customer or consumer. So, while marketing people today still give lip-service to the marketing concept and mouth Peter Drucker's words that "a company only exists to serve customers," in truth most are inwardly focused and financially driven. Many managers seem to believe that customers come as a result of marketing efforts to draw them in, rather than as a result of their product or service providing a customer benefit or value. We call the present marketing planning system used by both large and small organizations "Inside-Out." In other words, the planning is done on the basis of financial analysis with sales, marketing, and even profit goals set with an inside view. The litany goes something like this: "Here's what we manufacture. Here are the sales and profit goals we have set. Now, let's go out and find some customers who can help us make our goals." Exhibit 9-1 illustrates the common planning system used by most U.S. organizations today.

▼   *Exhibit 9-1*
Typical Inside-Out Planning Model

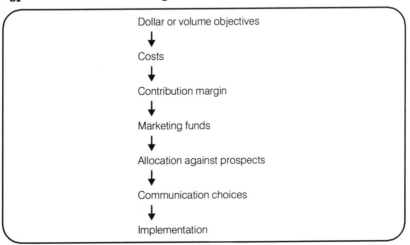

Dollar or volume objectives
↓
Costs
↓
Contribution margin
↓
Marketing funds
↓
Allocation against prospects
↓
Communication choices
↓
Implementation

It is this planning approach that results in the common view: "Here's what we want to do to those customers or prospects" rather than "Let's learn what customers and prospects want done to them." We believe it is this Inside-Out marketing and marketing communication planning that is responsible for many of today's unrealistic and ineffective marketing communications programs.

The IMC approach is to use "Outside-In" planning. That is, we start with customer or prospects. We then try to define what they want or need. Then, we match our products and services to those wants and needs. Developing communications programs for customers or prospects who really want or need your product or service is really more a question of getting the message to them, rather than trying to draw them in with clever creatives, mind-boggling discounts, or price cuts.

The Outside-In approach, which we propose and which is the heart of IMC, comes from the planning model that was discussed in some detail in Chapter 3. It is repeated as Exhibit 9-2 so you can contrast the IMC approach with the Inside-Out example in Exhibit 9-1.

Perhaps the best idea is to compare the IMC Outside-In approach with the way you presently plan marketing communications programs. Do you see a difference?

Organizational Structure as a Barrier to IMC

There is little doubt that organizational structures are one of the largest barriers to IMC in most organizations. Resistance to change can generally be overcome with time. The marketing planning system, with some thought and direction, can either evolve or be changed by executive fiat. Altering organizational structure, however, is a major undertaking.

Current Organizational Structure Problems

The internal structure of most U.S. organizations is a major hindrance to IMC for three basic reasons.

▼ **Exhibit 9-2**
IMC Planning Model

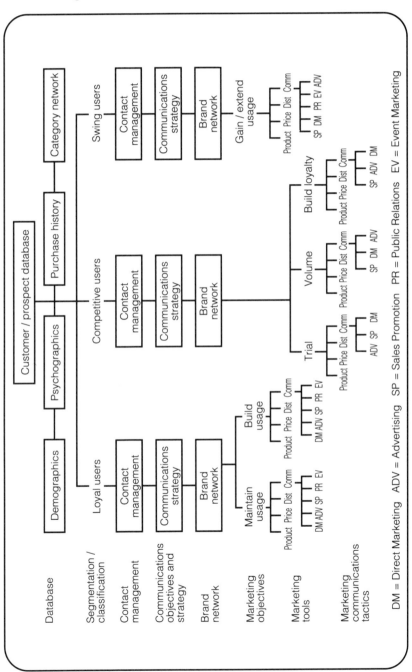

▼ *Exhibit 9-3*
Brand Management Organization

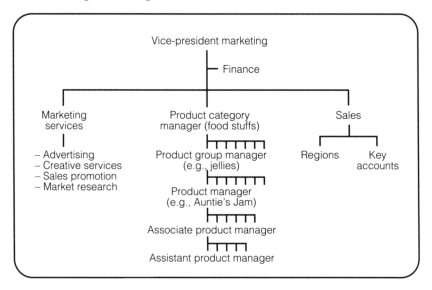

Communications Is a Low Priority in Most Marketing Organizations.

With few exceptions, marketing communications is not considered to be a very important task in most U.S. companies. If we look at a typical brand management organization, such as that illustrated in Exhibit 9-3, we find that the organization's communications are being developed and implemented at the lowest levels, that is, by the most junior and inexperienced employees. While it is true that top management often holds rights of approval over marketing communications programs, it is the brand manager and the assistant and associate brand manager who generally are developing the strategy and the communications programs.

The same is true in other organizational structures as well. Advertising or promotion managers are generally far down in the corporate pecking order. Where once advertising agencies met with and discussed communications strategies with the CEO of the marketing organizations, today they meet primarily with group or divisional managers or functional specialists.

The obvious implication of this structural location of the communications function is that top management doesn't consider it to be very important. Often that feeling is reinforced when the advertising or marketing communications budget is reduced or held in reserve in the fourth quarter of a company's fiscal year. If marketing communications is not very important, then holding back or cutting back is reasonable to the financially driven top managers.

Vertical Organizations Are the Norm in United States Companies, although Horizontal Structures Are Needed.

It has become increasingly clear that the vertical structures, primarily in the form of brand or product management systems, are largely responsible for the failure of marketing in the 1990s. Today, the consumer and the customer are focused more on a horizontal view of the marketplace. That is, they can find many substitutes for most products or services. For example, major competition for the frozen or microwavable dinners sold in supermarkets are fast foods items easily available from take-out restaurants. Consumers see these as being easily substituted for the store-bought items. They are all food. They are easy to get and easy to use. Yet, the organizational structure of the frozen dinner manufacturer forces the brand or product manager to focus his or her competitive marketing efforts against customers buying in the brand set. Thus, the major focus is on other frozen dinners.

The same vertical focus creates problems for the frozen dinner manufacturer's true customer—the supermarket owner. The supermarket owner considers the frozen dinner to be part of a larger category of frozen food. While the dinner manufacturer's brand manager is focused on getting more sales for his or her brand, the supermarket owner is looking at the entire category of frozen foods that must compete with fast food and take-out restaurants for consumer dollars. It is this narrow, vertical brand focus that is creating many of the problems for marketing organizations.

There is little question that brand management was a good idea for the 1950s and 1960s, and maybe even the early part of the 1970s. It seems, however, that brand management's narrow focus on only a single or a few brands, its short-term management orientation, and its heavy emphasis on microeconomic analysis are the major hinderances to many companies today. Certainly, brand management doesn't subscribe to most of the concepts we have developed 'earlier in this text. And, since communication is commonly a small part of the brand manager's responsibility, generally little is done in the way of planning or development of integrated marketing communications programs.

Functional Specialists Are Also a Major Hindrance to IMC

As business in the United States has become more complex, organizations have increasingly developed and relied upon functional specialists, i.e., advertising managers, direct marketing managers, sales promotion managers, events managers, and the like. While it is true that specialists are needed, they are a major hindrance to the concept of IMC. Specialists, by nature, are the ones who attempt to keep the communications programs separate. They are the ones who insist on obtaining and protecting separate budgets. It is only natural that a functional specialist believes that his or her specialty is the most important in the communication mix. Again, it is another case of Inside-Out focus that creates the problem.

The major problem is that many marketing organizations have begun to believe in the functional focus as well. If we look at the budgeting process, for example, commonly we find marketing funds are allocated by functional specialty, i.e., so much for advertising, so much for direct marketing, so much for public relations, and so on. Often, this allocation process is done with little or no regard for the communication needs of either the product or company, or the customers and prospects whom the communications programs are supposed to influence. Often this allocation process is based on historical precedents. This, then, forces the functional specialist to (a) argue for more funding to increase his or her influence and (b) spend the funds that have been allocated regardless of the communication needs of the organization simply to protect the allocation in the future.

Another major problem in most marketing organizations is that the functional specialists know only their own specialty. They know little about the other forms of communication or how they work or interact together. Today we have many functional specialists but very few communications generalists. IMC demands a broad view of communications and the specialists often can't provide that.

Some Organizational Solutions to IMC

Three basic organizational structural changes can be used to enable companies to practice IMC. They are (1) the establishment of a communications "czar," (2) restructuring the organization so that it is market-organized rather than brand-organized, and (3) making some basic revisions to traditional brand management. Each is discussed below.

Establishing a Communications "Czar."

The idea of centralized control would appear to be in direct conflict with today's management concept that attempts to push decision making as far down as possible in the organization, and closer to the customer. While this is a sound and needed management concept, problems occur when the communications function is broadly distributed throughout the organization and put in the hands of general marketing people who are commonly inexperienced in communications planning or implementation. Given existing communications systems, it is simply not practical or possible for communications to be planned or executed by every unit or business group. The brand has a certain meaning or value which must be maintained. For example, no one would think of giving a local retailer the authority to change, adapt, or re-invent the IBM logo. There must be some consistency across all media forms and across customer groups. That is not to say that local units cannot implement approved programs within certain guidelines. But it does mean there needs to be central control in the hands of communications generalists who can see and understand the total communications program for the organization and can therefore develop basic communications strategies and broad communications programs.

The most common approach in establishing a communications central authority is the use of a marketing communications structure or, as it is often called, a "marcom" manager. An example of the structure used by a telecommunications company is illustrated in Exhibit 9-4.

The marcom manager is the central controller of a broad array of communications specialists. Working in combination with the marketing manager, the marcom manager plans the overall communications program and initiates and controls the various types of marketing communications activities that are developed

▼ *Exhibit 9-4*

Marcom Management Structure

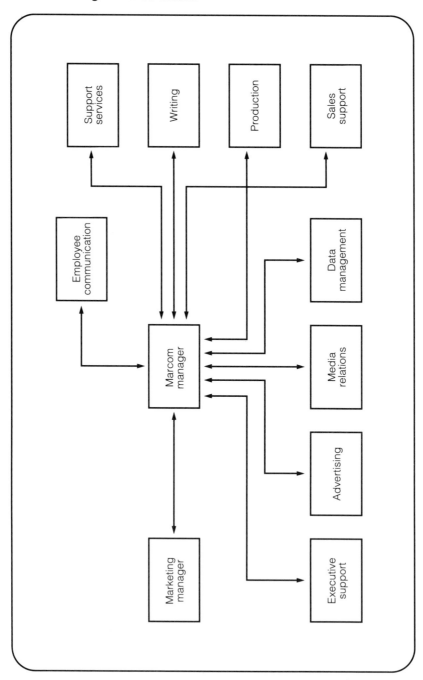

▼ **Exhibit 9-5**

Internal Relationship Manager

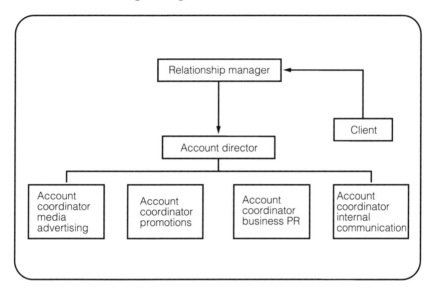

by the communications specialists. As can be seen in the company depicted in Exhibit 9-4, both internal and external communications are centralized under the marcom manager. Also note that the functional specialists report back to marketing management through the marcom manager. This assures that all communications programs have been coordinated and integrated.

In the marcom manager system, most of the communications programs are generated in house by a group of communications specialists. In other cases, the company may work with a group of outside specialists such as advertising or public relations agencies, sales promotion groups, and communications specialists. Examples of how these types of communications can be centralized and controlled are shown in Exhibits 9-5 and 9-6.

In Exhibit 9-5 the client has established a relationship manager within the organization. This relationship manager works with the marketing department and the account director of the various agencies or suppliers to develop an integrated plan. In most cases, the account director is employed by the agency (this works particularly well when the agencies are all under common ownership or management) and is the liaison between the various agencies and the marketing organization.

▼   *Exhibit 9-6*

Agency Relationship Manager

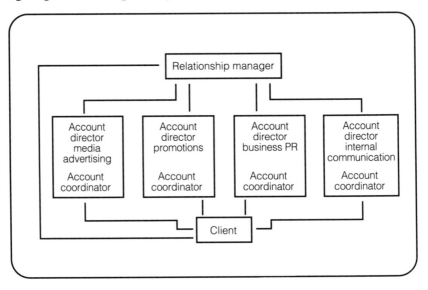

An alternative design is to have the relationship manager as an employee of the various supplier agencies. That approach is illustrated in Exhibit 9-6 below.

As can be seen, the marketing organization and the relationship manager both work with the outside suppliers (agencies in this case) to develop an integrated program. The client continues to have direct contact with the various functional groups to guide and direct their activities. At the same time, the relationship manager works from the inside of the agency organization to coordinate the activities of the various groups. Both these organizational structures have strengths and weaknesses. Which would work best depends on the relationship between the marketing organization and its suppliers.

This centralized approach, with the establishment of a communications czar, assumes that the existing organization will not be changed. This is simply a consolidation of the communications function into one person or group. Thus, this structure is fairly easy to implement, although there are inherent problems brought about by the existing organizational structures. It does, however, initiate the process of centralization, which can then lead to integration of the organization's communications activities.

Restructuring the Organization to Become Market-Organized Rather than Brand-Organized.

The second approach to IMC implementation involves some rather dramatic changes to the existing brand or product management system. Chiefly, it involves moving from a brand-focused to a customer-focused structure. That is, the company becomes externally rather than internally focused. While it sounds like something that every organization should be doing, it is a dramatic change from the traditional brand management approach.

An example of a market-focused organization is illustrated in Exhibit 9-7.

The main change in the structure of a market-oriented company from a brand-oriented organization is that the focus of the company is on the customer or prospect, not the brand or the marketing company. For example, in a market-organized company the emphasis would be on how customers and consumers view the products, i.e., how they use them, how they think about them, how they purchase them, not on how the company manufactures them. An example will help illustrate the difference.

Assume Acme Company is a widely diversified food manufacturing and processing company with a brand management structure. Currently, they have a line of cookies, a line of potato and corn chips, a line of refrigerated dips, and a subsidiary company that manufactures and markets candy bars. In this example, Acme would believe it was competing in the cookie category, the chip category, the dairy category and the candy category. Yet, from the consumer's view, all the products are probably considered some sort of snack food. They are often used at the same time and perhaps even for the same purpose. Here we see the problem of vertical structures for a horizontal consumer product market.

Under the market-organized structure, Acme would create a "snack foods group" to serve the snack food segment of the consumer marketplace. This group, shown as the market segment in Exhibit 9-7, would be responsible for the marketing of the entire line of snack food products. Supporting that group would be a marketing services department that would provide the functional expertise needed and a special product manager group that would be responsible for new snack food product development. The sales force would be on the same level as the market segment managers, so they would work in combination to develop the most effective marketing/sales program possible.

▼ **Exhibit 9-7**
Market Focused Organization

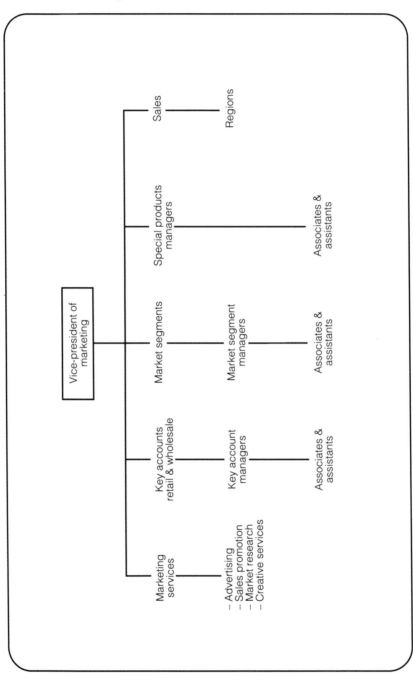

▼   *Exhibit 9-8*

Market Segment Management

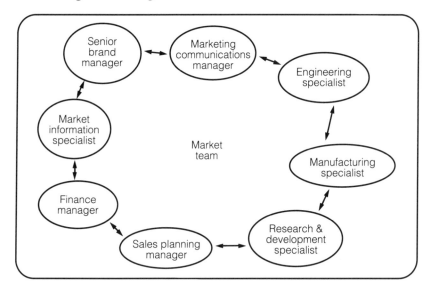

In addition, this structure allows the marketer to recognize the growing importance of specific major customers through the use of a key account manager for both retail and wholesale. This group would be responsible for working with the major retail customers of the organization to make sure that the marketing programs are well organized and implemented.

It would be within the market segment group that the integrated marketing communications program would be developed. Illustrated in Exhibit 9-8 is the new "team" approach to market segment marketing.

The team consists of a number of specialists who focus on a group of products. It includes all the functional specialists required to manage the brands that are in the market segment. Depending on the demands of the brands being managed, the group can be expanded or reduced to include other functional specialists are well. The critical change in this approach is that the members of the team rotate through the group rather than shift from brand to brand or group to group. That way, expertise in the market and the brands can be developed by the team members. Marketing communications is the responsibility of the group, although there is a marketing communications specialist. With this approach, the group plans and coordinates all the marketing communications for the brands that it ~~presents to all the markets it serves. This team approach can easily accommodate the use of outside functional expert groups such as advertising, public relations, or sales promotion agencies. The control is within the group that is responsible for both external and internal communications for the market segment and the brands included in the group.

This approach is the most radical of those that we propose but it does guarantee that the focus of the organization is on the customer and the consumer, not on the brand or the organization. It assures the use of Outside-In planning in all areas of the company's operations.

Implementing Revisions to Brand Management

A number of organizations have recognized the inherent myopic view of the brand management system and have initiated adaptations or changes. In Exhibit 9-9 we illustrate the arrangement that appears to have the most potential.

▼   *Exhibit 9-9*

Revision to Brand Management

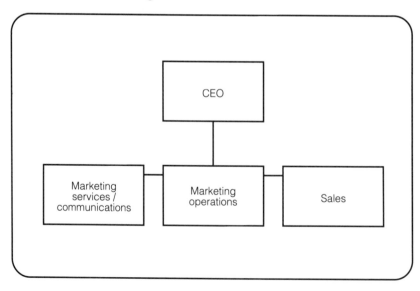

In this structure, all the layers of middle management (division managers, group managers, category managers, and so on) have been stripped away. There is a direct relationship between the marketing managers and the CEO. This simplified structure has only three groups, each headed by a manager. Thus, the managers of the marketing services/communications group, the marketing operations group, and sales, plus the CEO, make up the management team. It is the marketing services/communications group in which we are most interested, but to understand how that group works we must first understand the marketing operations and sales groups.

Sales is responsible for the sale of the product to the customer base. This group is the face-to-face contact with the customer. Marketing operations is responsible for all manufacturing and production of the product. This group brings the product to the shipping dock. There, marketing services/communications takes over.

Marketing services/communications consists of three groups as shown in Exhibit 9-10.

▼ **Exhibit 9-10**
Marketing Services/Communications

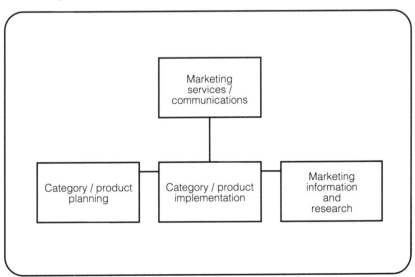

The category/product planning group is responsible for the long-term planning and strategic development of the brand or group of brands. Their view is three to five years out. The category/product implementation group is responsible for the ongoing, day-to-day marketing and communications activities in the marketplace. The marketing information and research group is responsible for all market, consumer, and retail information that the groups need. It is also their responsibility to set up measurement systems to determine the success of the various programs that are planned and implemented. The category/product planning group, the category/product implementation group, and the marketing information and research group work together to develop the annual marketing and communications plan. However, it is the responsibility of the category/product implementation group to execute that plan. Therefore, all outside suppliers report to the implementation group as they handle the day-to-day activities on the brand.

All marketing activities, including all types of communication for the category and the brands, are centralized in the implementation group. Thus, they are able to develop IMC programs with little difficulty. In addition, since the groups are focused on categories, the necessary Outside-In view always prevails.

We now move to the last barrier to IMC planning in the organization: capability, control, and commitment.

Capability, Control, and Commitment
The Question is Capability

The decentralized nature of the marketing communications business also has much to do with the resistance to IMC. Everyone wants to believe that his or her product is different, the market is unique, or only local response to the marketplace is effective. In addition, large marketing organizations have tended to rely on outside entities such as advertising or public relations agencies, sales promotion suppliers, events organizers and the like to provide them with the marketing communications tactics they traditionally have used. Today, as the marketplace has become more sophisticated and the communications alternatives have multiplied, the question of who does the communications planning has become a major one in many marketing organizations.

In the heyday of the mass media, the 1950s until the late 1970s, much of the marketing communications planning was done through a cooperative effort between the marketing organization and its agency representatives. Increasingly, however, in the 1980s the marketing organizations began to do more and more of the planning internally. This seemed like a natural thing to do as the analytical skills of marketing professionals developed and sophisticated financial tracking systems were installed. Throughout the decade, as marketing organizations did more and more of the general planning, the outside agencies and other suppliers did less and less. Today, many advertising agencies have become simply vendors rather than partners with their clients. Thus, as the marketing and marketing communications planning has been drawn in house, marketing organizations have become less and less inclined to share data, information or material with their outside suppliers. So rather than having another, perhaps broader view of the marketplace through their agencies or other marketing communications suppliers, the marketing organizations in the United States have become more and more myopic and indulged in tunnel vision.

The advertising agencies responded to this internal control of the planning process by dismantling their research operations. Why, they reasoned, if the marketer is going to do the research and analysis, do we need any research people? While this centralization process does form a locus of information and market knowledge within the marketing organization, it is beset by the same problems that affect brand management systems and functional specialists, as was discussed in the earlier section.

The Problem Is Information

The major problem that most marketing organizations face is the burgeoning amount of marketplace information. Where once the challenge of the marketing manager was to get information on which to make a decision, today the issue is more of sorting through the data trying to make sense of it. Scanners and other electronic marketing data gathering systems, the rapid rise of the computer and data analysis in the marketing department, and the flood of information from myriad sources on the consumer, the retailer, and the marketplace has inundated most marketing organizations.

At the same time that information has been proliferating, there has been a change in the source of much market data. Traditionally the manufacturing organization generated the data and did the analysis, or it was collected and analyzed by outside market research suppliers. Today, however, much of what we know about what is selling, what marketing programs are successful, and what marketing communications programs seem to be having some effect comes not from the manufacturer but from the retailer. The information power in the marketplace has shifted from the manufacturer to the retailer. Since traditionally there has been an adversarial relationship between the manufacturer and the retailer, this shift in the source of information and power in the channels will have much to do with how marketing organizations develop their IMC programs. As a start, we are seeing more marketing organizations develop their own customer databases. These organizations are attempting to develop customer and prospect files and to create marketing communications programs to reach and influence their specific customers and prospects. As marketing organizations become more skilled at database marketing, they will likely become more skilled at the tasks that are required to develop IMC programs. The problem exists, however, for those organizations that are not so enlightened or whose management has not seen the need for a proprietary database.

The Concern Is the Cost of Database Marketing

There is little question that a customer and prospect database is or will be critical to the success of the marketing organization in the future. The problem is: Database marketing is a substantial and ongoing fixed investment for the company. In today's economic climate, investing in a database is a major decision for the organization. To many marketing managers and even CEOs, it seems much more reasonable to attempt to compete in the marketplace with mass market techniques such as sales promotion, direct marketing, and events, all of which can be classified as variable costs, rather than to incur the fixed and continuing costs of developing a customer database.

The Payoff Is Evaluation

Part of the difficulty in convincing management to invest in a database is the question of how marketing activities are evaluated. Traditionally, most organizations have viewed the cost of message distribution as the critical variable in the marketing communications program, i.e., the medium that could deliver the most messages at the lowest possible cost was considered the best choice. Today, particularly with IMC, our view is changing. We are more interested in the effect of the messages that were delivered than in the cost of delivery. Therefore, as we move into behavioral segmentation and measuring the marketplace effects of marketing communications rather than the attitudinal responses, a database will become increasingly important. And, as costs decline as a result of technology it will become feasible for all organizations to have a database and control of their own sources of information. As this occurs, the barriers to IMC will decline or disappear. In the meantime, however, the lack of a database and the resulting information that can be obtained from that source will continue to be a major barrier to the development of integrated marketing communications programs.

Having completed this look at the barriers that face the organization trying to implement an IMC program and some possible solutions, we now turn to the basic requirements for the development of an IMC program.

Basic Requirements to Overcome the Barriers to IMC

While there are several barriers to an IMC program, and these will vary based on the type and kind of organization, there are four factors that we believe are mandatory for success. They are listed and described below.

Mandatory Factor One: IMC Must Start at the Top

Regardless of the organization, its structure or the type of business, for an IMC program to be successful it must start at the top management level and filter down through the organization. It cannot start at the middle or at the bottom and work its way up.

Top-down direction and commitment is vital. The CEO must actively support IMC. He or she must remove the many barriers that will prevent the implementation of IMC. That means not just financial support but aggressive internal support in the form of directives, memos, and in some cases even cheerleading. It must be clear to every employee that IMC is vital and is supported at the top if it is to succeed.

Mandatory Factor Two: Customer-Focused Marketing

For IMC to work, the organization must commit to the customer. It must identify, learn about, work with, and be concerned with customers at all times and at all levels. It must refocus its energies on locating and satisfying customers rather than just making products or providing services. It must adjust marketing programs to make them customer friendly and customer active. Most of all, it must commit to the Peter Drucker principle: The company is in business to build and satisfy customers. That will be a major change for most marketing organizations but it is necessary for IMC to succeed.

Mandatory Factor Three: Communication Must Become a Sustainable Competitive Advantage

For IMC to succeed, the total organization must recognize that communications will be one of its most important competitive weapons. When products are at parity, distribution is similar, pricing is equal, and high levels of customer service are common, then the only competitive weapon the marketer has at his or her disposal is communications and relationships with customers. Indeed, communication can and must become the sustainable competitive advantage that the organization uses to remain a viable factor in the marketplace. This requires new thinking and a new understanding of communication by all levels of management but it is a must if the organization is to succeed.

Mandatory Factor Four: Communications Must Be Centralized

While decentralization of management is critical to being competitive in today's marketplace, the centralization or consolidation of the communications function is necessary. There must be a broad view of communications and well-defined and well-established strategies to build and protect the brands the company markets. This cannot be done on a decentralized basis. In any organization, the communications function must be retained by the corporate leadership and it must be viewed as one of the major activities of that group just as financial or other corporate functions. Local implementation of well-planned and well-organized communications strategies are possible, but there can be little question that communications must be in the hands of generalists with a broad view of the entire corporate operation. The communications program must be orchestrated so that a clear, concise relationship is built with each individual customer. Communication in the 1990s is too important to put in the hands of unskilled managers or low-level employees, for it is the very future of the organization.

Two Case Histories: Does Integrated Marketing Communications Really Work?

▼

From a logical standpoint, IMC should work. After all, what you are doing is saying the right thing to the right person at the right time. How can you miss?

The authors reviewed dozens of case histories that proved this new way of thinking produces desired behavior. We have chosen two cases for this chapter because they present particularly difficult problems that were solved by the IMC approach. The first describes a problem faced by a well-known philanthropic organization, the second is a business-to-business case.

The American Cancer Society

Integrated marketing communications is a thinking process that works in every type of business category. It even works in the area of public service, where so often charity organizations are solely dependent on traditional media for exposure of their messages. The following is an example of an IMC campaign developed by the American Cancer Society. The authors participated in its development and execution and were first-hand witnesses to a unique success story.

The American Cancer Society (ACS) is one of America's leading philanthropic organizations. Its work in research, education, and service is helping us all fight and control cancer. In order to function at all, the society depends on communication to its various publics: the cancer sufferer, doctors, nurses, legislators, and all those people who can reduce their risk of getting cancer by taking advantage of early detection and prevention methods. If the society does not do an effective job of communication, society as a whole will suffer.

The communication challenge is complicated by two facts. First, the ACS is made up of distinct departments—medical, research, education, service, prevention, early detection—each with its own target audience, each sending out a message of its own.

The second complication is that the ACS does not run paid advertising. It is all placed as a public service by the media. As a result, ACS cannot run what would normally be an effective media campaign with sufficient reach and frequency to make an impression on the market. Even in the areas of public relations and distribution of collateral materials like posters and brochures, the society does not have adequate resources to do a proper job. When the departments within the society tend to execute separate materials at different times, communication becomes totally uncoordinated and, therefore, far less productive.

Communication is the energy that drives various functions of the ACS. Communication can actually save lives. Yet the ACS has found it difficult to communicate because of a departmentalized organization and a necessary reliance on voluntarily placed public service advertising and promotion.

With this perplexing problem in mind, the ACS communications department in Illinois appointed an integrated advertising/ marketing communications company to devise an integrated strategy. The communications company was DDB Needham in Chicago. This organization of 650 experts includes strategic generalists, advertising professionals, and two specific sister companies: Porter Novelli, a specialist in public relations; and Rapp Collins Marcoa, a company that specializes in direct marketing. A team of creative research and account management people from each discipline was put together along with members of the communications committee of the Illinois division of the American Cancer Society.

The assignment was simple: develop a continuing, integrated marketing communications campaign that would help save the lives of those who, through lack of information of how to prevent the disease, would die of skin cancer.

▼   *Exhibit 10-1*

Incidence of Skin Cancer

Source: American Cancer Society, *Cancer Guide, 1991, Facts and Figures.*

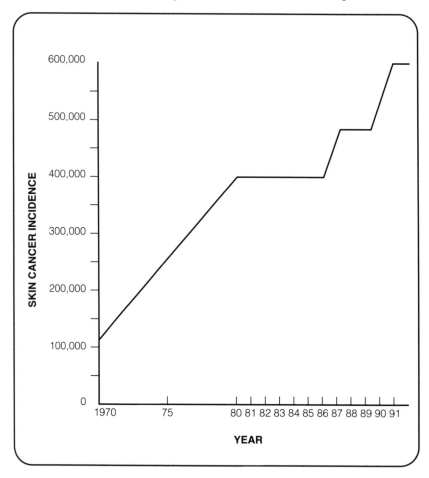

The skin cancer incidence in the United States is alarming—600,000 new cases per year; 8,800 deaths per year. (See Exhibits 10-1 and 10-2.) If the long-term trend were not contained, it could reach epidemic proportions.

What causes the disease? Overexposure to the sun. Who has the problem? Mainly those who spend a lot of time in the sun, usually having acquired the tanning habit in their teens.

The solution to the problem? Communicate the fact that a suntan lotion with sun protection factor (SPF) rating of 15 or more

▼ **Exhibit 10-2**
Incidence of Death from Skin Cancer
Source: American Cancer Society.

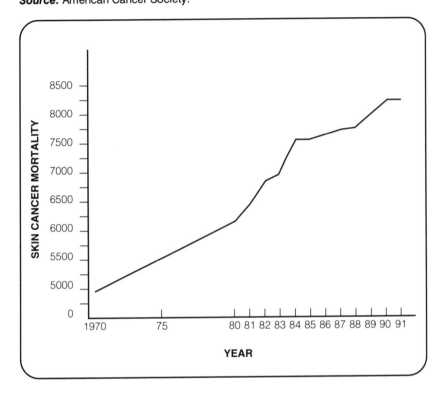

can help prevent the disease when applied before exposure. SPF allows you to spend more time in the sun without damaging your skin. For example, if you usually can tolerate exposure to the sun for one minute without protection, using a suntan lotion with an SPF of 15 allows you 15 minutes of exposure. You may ask why the manufacturers of suntan lotions did not promote a product with SPF 15 already. The ACS investigation showed that it was an expensive educational job for the lotion makers to undertake, and the manufacturers decided to wait until they could use their dollars for advertising rather than educating.

The Illinois division of the ACS undertook the job as part of their mission. It seemed like a relatively simple communication challenge: Use this product and save your life. What a promise! You can't be more end-benefit oriented. Everyone at the ACS—doctors, health administrators, medical researchers—agreed. Even the communications agency agreed. "Save your life!" What a selling line. You can't miss.

But the main principle of integrated marketing communications was being totally avoided. The ACS was about to make a decision like so many manufacturers make, a decision based on what they thought rather than on what the *consumer thinks* and wants and needs. The ACS was thinking from inside out instead of outside in. Thank goodness someone among the vast army of communications experts involved said, "Why don't we talk to the potential user?" Must you talk to the potential user when the benefit is so obvious? This suntan lotion with SPF 15 can save your life.

Well, the ACS did talk to the potential consumer: young women and men between the ages of 12 and 18. And guess what? They thought they were immortal. The idea of saving their lives at their young age was relatively unimportant, especially when compared with what to them was the bigger benefit of the sun: making you more attractive to the opposite sex.

The consumers were describing what they thought their needs were, not what the ACS thought their needs were. And the ACS began to listen. What they heard was that consumers will buy a product that lets them look more attractive because it safely lets you stay in the sun longer. That idea is far different from "saving lives."

By listening to the consumer and not to its biases, the ACS took the first step toward integrated marketing communications that would eventually establish a dialogue with the consumers based on *their* needs and lifestyles.

The next thing that was vital for the integrated marketing communications committee was to further refine and define the target audience. Keep in mind, the committee did not have paid advertising as a resource. It could not count on delivering frequent messages to the potential user.

The integrated communications assignment was to create an impact with everyone who could affect the sale of the product, although the ACS was not the actual seller of suntan lotion. The audience was divided into five groups. Each group had a specific buying incentive; each group could affect the eventual sale.

Group One: The manufacturers of the product, the various retailers, category trade organizations, wholesalers, and brokers.

Their buying incentives were obviously a new and more profitable form of suntan lotion and potentially greater use of suntan lotion resulting in more profits.

Group Two: General medical practitioners, dermatologists, nurses, and pharmacists. Their buying incentive was to help prevent their clients from getting cancer.

Group Three: Lifeguards, gym teachers, tennis coaches, barbers, etc. Among this group, the buying incentive also was to help their "clients" safely enjoy the sun.

Group Four: Parents of the potential users. Here, too, the buying incentive was to help their children safely enjoy the sun.

Group Five: The potential users—men and women between the ages of 12 and 18. Here, the buying incentive was a bit more overt: You can look more attractive to the opposite sex by safely staying out in the sun longer.

In addition to discovering the buying incentive, by talking to each of these groups the ACS learned how to reach them most effectively. The ACS found out how they buy, how they use the product, what media they are exposed to throughout the day and on vacations and weekends, and what was the best time to talk to these people when their minds were closest to the product concept.

The media to be used on Group I was personal contact with the communications committee representatives. To dramatize the benefit of profits to be made from distributing and selling suntan lotion with an SPF of 15 or more, the ACS offered an SPF 15/ACS seal that could be used on the package and at the point of sale. (See Exhibit 10-3.)

The ACS also offered to distribute product samples and introductory promotions in its collateral material. In return for this, the manufacturer would underwrite the cost of the collateral pieces.

The IMC committee analyzed every possible way of reaching the vital Group V. The potential users' daily activities were mapped. The committee investigated where they were and what they did from the time they woke up in the morning until they went to bed at night. Contact occasions based on when the users thought of the sun and all of the pleasures connected with the sun were also investigated. The first thought was not mass media. (However, TV and radio commercials and print ads were eventually developed

▼   **Exhibit 10-3**

SPF/ACS Product Seal

for use in public service announcements.) The list below shows some of the media considered and eventually used to reach Group V.

Group V	**"Contacts"**
Potential User:	Posters for home
men, women; 12–18 years	Posters for school
Buying incentive:	MTV
You can look more attractive to the	Radio
opposite sex by safely staying in the	TV
sun longer.	Newspaper/magazine
	advertisements
	News conference
	Skywriting
	T-shirts
	Bathing caps
	Sunglasses
	Brochures

Similar analyses were made of the most fruitful ways of reaching Groups II, III and IV. Among the media chosen were brochures, direct mail, videotapes, posters, informational pamphlets, news programs, and interview shows.

The strategy was sound. What was needed was a creative execution of the strategy that caught people's attention, an execution that delivered and dramatized the benefit of SPF 15 but, beyond that, got people talking and buying—an execution so powerful that all target groups would instantly relate. Ideally, the theme used should even excite the consumer press and trade press, doctors, nurses, retailers, and parents. (See Exhibit 10-4.)

That was a tall order, but if such a theme could be developed it would almost ensure the success of the integrated marketing communications program behind the SPF 15 concept.

At this point, the challenge of creating such a theme was given to the integrated creative group at DDB Needham.

The creative group searched for a selling idea that would:

1 dramatize the benefit of SPF 15 with a memorable selling idea

2 be relevant to the potential user

3 surprise the target and produce word-of-mouth communication about the product concept.

▼   *Exhibit 10-4*

The ACS Integrated Marketing Communications Plan

	Advertising	Public Relations	Sales Promotions	Direct Response
Health Objective	Encourage people to avoid sunburn			
Target	Sun worshippers	1. Moms 2. Teens 3. Trade association/ manufacturers 4. Health professionals 5. Clubs 6. Schools		

Purpose	Use SPF 15+	1. Encourage family
		   use
		2. Use
		3. Disseminate P-O-P
		4–6. Encourage
		   client/customer
		   use		

Promise	Be more attractive to opposite sex by safely staying out in the sun longer	1. Confident protecting
		   family health
		2. Enjoy sun
		3. Sales up
		4–6. Impact preventive
		   health		

Support	– SPF 15+ blocks
	   most harmful sun
	– ACS authority
		– Medical studies
		– Consumer sales
		   trend
		– ACS cooperation		

Personality	Healthy Effective Savvy Fun Contemporary			
Aperture	Pre/early tanning season (some continuous)			
	Beaches, parks			

Consumer "Contact" Points	TV PSA
	Radio PSA
	Print PSA
	MTV
	Transit
	Billboards
	Skywriting
	Newspaper
	Wall posters
		1. Editorial
		2. School
		   – Special events
		   – Spokesperson
		3. Universal symbol
		4. Brochure
		   – Curriculum guide
		   – Poster
		5. Media publicity
		   (various targets)
			– Coupon with mail-in
			– Sports tie-in
			– Samples/airlines
			– Displays with
			   leave-behinds, etc.
				– Brochure with
				   coupon
				– Sunscreen novelty
				   mail-in

The DDB Needham group came up with a great idea. To dramatize the good looks that can safely be obtained by using a suntan lotion with an SPF of 15, use the endorsement of the models from the annual *Sports Illustrated* bathing suit issue. The models actually used suntan lotion with an SPF of 15.

These models visually dramatize the idea of the message that you can safely stay out in the sun and look good. The DDB Needham creative group went one step further. They created a selling line that tied in directly with the point the strategy was trying to make. These models were more than a "10"—the popular denominator for good looks. These models were "Definitely a 15." This selling line was a memorable promise to the consumer that tied directly to the product attribute.

Following are examples of the materials produced. The key pieces were "Definitely a 15" posters given away to potential users. More than 75,000 of these posters were ordered the first year in Chicago, and new orders continued coming in every day.

The campaign was launched in Chicago at a news conference with every media outlet in the area attending. The launch pointed out the potential dangers of skin cancer and introduced the new campaign to help combat it.

The campaign received coverage in all newspapers, three minutes or more of news on all prime-time TV stations, radio news programs, and interviews galore.

Brochures were requested by mail, while posters, samples, and informational pamphlets were in demand—especially from the Group V potential user.

This was an integrated effort. The prevention, early detection, medical, and educational arms of the ACS all successfully participated. The manufacturers who made the product and the retailers who sold the product began to cooperate. Even the medical community and school administrations joined in the effort.

The greatest testament to the success of the campaign is that it is now going into its third year. More and more manufacturers and retailers are selling suntan lotion with an SPF of 15 or more. And even more vital, the potential target is becoming a user and believer in the product benefit. The ACS, through integrated marketing communications, has led the way to the successful introduction of a new product category that will probably save millions of lives.

▼   *Exhibit 10-5*
"Definitely a 15" Marketing Pieces

▼ *Exhibit 10-5 continued*

AT 2, SHE'S ALREADY A 15.

USE A SUNSCREEN
OF SPF 15. GIVE
YOURSELF THE CHANCE
OF A LIFETIME.

**AMERICAN
CANCER
SOCIETY**®

For more information on skin protection and coupons good for discounts on SPF 15 products call **1-800-ACS-2345.**

▼ *Exhibit 10-5 continued*

▼　**Exhibit 10-5 *(continued)***

American Cancer Society
Sunscreen 15
:30 TV

 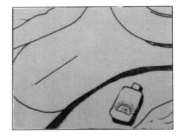

AVO:　　The Sports Illustrated
　　　　Swimsuit models

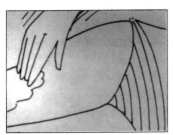 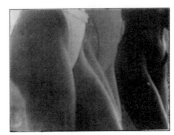

Every single one is definitely　　because each and every one
a 15

▼ *Exhibit 10-5 (continued)*

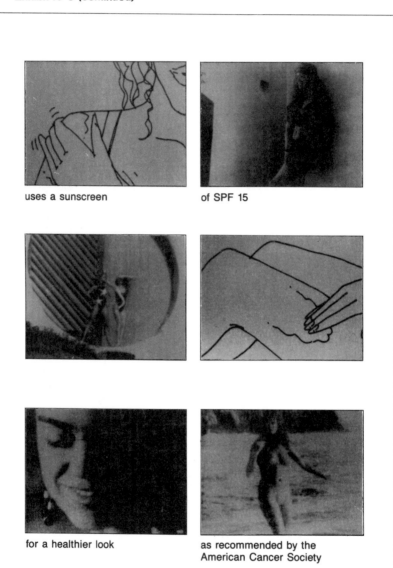

uses a sunscreen

of SPF 15

for a healthier look

as recommended by the
American Cancer Society

▼ **Exhibit 10-5 *(continued)***

It's the clear-cut answer

to helping prevent skin cancer

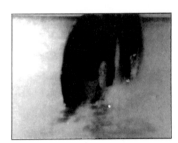

SUPER: Use sunscreen SPF 15.
GIVE YOURSELF THE
CHANCE OF A LIFETIME.

The integrated marketing communications campaign has helped unite the ACS internally and ultimately produced an external message that effectively accomplished the society's goal to benefit humanity.

The Milk Carton Case

A significant business problem, one that will not yield to a conventional (and yes, "safe") solution, is usually the precursor to significant business success. Just such a problem faced International Paper and other producers of paperboard milk cartons at the dawn of the 1980s. Paper companies make money by chemically extracting fiber from trees and reconstituting that fiber into added-value end products ranging from newsprint to sophisticated engineered packaging board. How much money a company makes is a complex equation, trading off factors such as the cost of its fiber source, the cost of its extraction process, and the costs of manufacturing and marketing its paper or paperboard products against the value the market places on those products.

The cost of manufacturing a product such as bleached board (the base stock for both the manila folders you probably have a dozen of in your desk drawer and the milk carton you may have had on your breakfast table) does not vary significantly no matter what end use the board is sold for. However, what the company gets for the board can vary by a factor of ten, depending on the end use. Therefore, assuming constant cost control and a supply/demand equilibrium, a company's ability to sell into higher-value end-use markets can be the single most important determinant of its profitability.

It is also important to note that paper is a capital-intensive industry. A mill built today will have a price tag in the neighborhood of a billion dollars. The only way to amortize this investment on a reasonable schedule (and the only way to run any process efficiently) is to run the mill 24 hours a day, seven days a week, 50 weeks a year. Out the back end comes roll after thousand-pound roll of paper or paperboard, earmarked for customers who will pay prices for it in direct proportion to the market value of the products they will produce from it, tempered by the law of supply and demand. Healthy high-value end-use market demand makes for happy paper company shareowners. Erosion of high-end markets causes depression, in more ways than one.

The mood was gloomy among some members of the Paperboard Packaging Council (PPC) in early 1980. The PPC is a Washington, D.C.-based association whose corporate members included at the time the "Big Five" paper companies that produced bleached board for dairy product packaging—Champion International, International Paper (IP), Potlatch, Westvaco, and Weyerhauser. They and smaller companies account for tons of paperboard packaging a year, for everything from toothpaste to Tonka toys, Cracker Jack to Jack Daniels, Maybelline to McDLTs.

The single biggest domestic consumer of that board, however, was the dairy industry, and the single product accounting for the largest share of that consumption was milk. In 1980, the U.S. dairy industry put six billion paperboard milk cartons on breakfast tables across the country.

But the trend was ominous. By 1970, paperboard had climbed to an 80 percent share of the milk packaging market, with blow-molded plastic and dwindling glass splitting the rest of the market about evenly. A profound change had taken place in the previous two decades in how Americans got their milk, from home delivery to purchasing at the supermarket.

Over the next decade, however, a different piper came to call the tune and the new music wasn't to the taste of the paper companies. When dairies delivered milk door to door, dairies made their own decisions about how they would package the milk. Paper was lighter in weight, more space-efficient, and cheaper than glass. Paper required less storage space initially, and allowed dairies to eliminate the whole return, wash, and resterilize operation. When distribution first began to shift to the supermarket, those benefits became even more important. In fact, dairies even got a bonus with paper, the ability to promote their own name and other products, such as ice cream and cottage cheese, on the side panels. Paper companies had no problem ousting glass as the chief container material and set up their sales forces to compete with the only threat they could see for a given dairy's business—each other.

While paper company salespeople worked to persuade dairy production and quality control people that their company's board would run more smoothly, have fewer defects, and print more consistently than another company's product, dairy marketing people were getting a more powerful message from their own customers.

"Supply our milk," said supermarket dairy product purchasers, "in gallon-sized blow-molded plastic jugs."

There were reasons for this change. Plastic jugs had handles and were easier and quicker to stock in dairy cases. Plastic jugs rarely leaked as paperboard cartons sometimes did, and "leakers" created a mess to clean up—expensive, odiferous, even a health hazard.

Most important, plastic jugs were gallon-sized. Supermarkets knew that the number one reason a consumer would visit their most nettlesome competitor—the convenience store—was because she had run out of milk. Worse yet, while the customer was in the store, she (or he) would also buy some of the high-profit impulse items such as snack foods that supermarkets count on to offset their slim margins on staples and basic grocery products.

So supermarkets wanted to load up the consumer with milk by the gallon, often loss-leader priced, to keep him or her from making those in-between shopping trips.

The consumer, too, had reasons to prefer plastic. She preferred to buy milk for the family in large quantities, especially when a bargain was offered. She liked to be able to see through the translucent jug and know how much milk was left. The handle made it easier for the kids to manage and pour the milk. The customer had seen more than one carton slip out of someone's little hands, flooding the kitchen floor.

The dairy had little reason to resist the pressure. If the owner had invested $600,000 in a blow-molding machine, he had his investment to work off. Even if he bought jugs from an outside supplier, the cost was often lower than that of paper cartons. The plastic resin, after all, was a byproduct of the petroleum refining process, plentiful and cheap. So while the paper companies fought among themselves for share, the pie got smaller and smaller. By 1980, the most successful company, International Paper, held (by one estimate) 47 percent of the paperboard milk packaging market, but paperboard's share of milk packaging was down to 40 percent and falling.

Here, then, was a difficult business problem. The company's direct customer, the dairy, wanted to buy less, not more of its product. It didn't matter that IP's quality program had virtually eliminated the "leakers" and had greatly improved the printing surface.

The customer's customer, the supermarket, didn't want the product. The customer's customer's customer, the consumer, didn't want the product. On the Boston Consulting Group (BCG) strategic planning grid, this business looked like a cash cow at best, on its way to becoming a dog. "Harvest," the experts would say. "Divest, if you can find a buyer."

There was one problem, however. Companies such as International Paper had several billion dollars invested in paperboard mills that were spewing out hundreds of tons of the board every day, seven days a week, 50 weeks a year. They couldn't just let the material pile up in warehouses full to the ceiling with giant rolls; no money would come in until the board was sold. If the company abandoned this profitable, high-volume end use and the market were allowed to melt away, what could IP do with all this stuff—dump it into lower-value end markets for conversion into, for example, manila folders? The difference in revenue would have been $200 a ton at then-current prices, and the contribution quickly would have dropped even further as the additional 30–40 thousand tons per year of product available for this purpose oversaturated that hardly robust market.

True, looking five years down the road, there was light at the end of the tunnel. A new, even higher-value end use was appearing, special, highly-engineered multi-ply cartons for fresh orange juice, such as those used by Tropicana's Pure Premium and Procter & Gamble's Citrus Hill. The problem was how to create a bridge between previous and new uses, how to keep the shareholders from getting restless.

It is said that business problems belong to those who can solve them. This one, perhaps by default, gravitated toward people in communications. Although the paper company's trade sales and marketing efforts had produced significant competitive share gains, the company was powerless to halt the inexorable decline of the market itself. Could marketing communications help? Maybe.

Step One toward solving the business dilemma was the formation of a master task force by International Paper to define the problem. Included were the aggressive general manager of the converting business (the interim customer which actually purchased the board from the mills and turned it into printed milk carton blanks), the manager of market research and strategic planning for paperboard packaging, the marketing and sales managers, the product manager, IP's corporate vice president of marketing services, the director of corporate advertising and marketing communications, and the managers of marketing publicity and promotion.

Importantly, two people from International Paper's advertising agency, Ogilvy & Mather—the management supervisor and the creative director—were also members of the task force from the beginning. Others, notably people from Ogilvy & Mather's public relations, merchandising, and direct marketing operations, were added soon after.

Step Two was the identification of the leverage point. Dairies could only be influenced by their customers, the supermarkets. Supermarkets in turn could only be influenced by consumers. If it were possible to convince the consumer that paperboard cartons were superior in some way to plastic jugs for milk packaging, the consumer might demand that supermarkets provide milk in paper. The stores in turn would demand a shift back to paper from their dairies, reversing the decline. International Paper, by dint of its superior market share, would benefit disproportionately; therefore, International Paper decided it would take a leadership role and work to develop a solution on its own.

Step Three was to identify and thoroughly analyze the target consumer. Who buys milk, and why? What beliefs and attitudes does the buyer (usually a woman as it turned out) have, what wants and needs might create an opportunity to open a dialogue about paper cartons versus plastic jugs?

Secondary research, such as Simmons Market Research Bureau data, showed that the familar 80/20 phenomenon was present in this case, too. More than 80 percent of all milk sold was bought by a core group of mothers between the ages of 25 and 44 who had children between the ages of 6 and 18 living at home. These women bought milk in large quantities, which also explains the supermarkets' preference for gallon-sized containers. They encouraged their children to drink milk because they believed, deeply and unshakably, that milk was good for kids.

Qualitative research probing showed that the belief that milk was "good for kids" meant that it had vitamins and minerals, that it helped kids grow, that it helped build strong bones and teeth. Mothers perceived milk as "almost the perfect food." However, some women (particularly the better-educated among them and mothers who lived in the West) were concerned about milk's fat content and tended to purchase 2 percent, 1 percent or even skim milk.

International Paper's product development engineers were brought into the task force to work on the problem of gallon size, while the research lab scientists and food-handling specialists were assigned to explore the relationship between packaging and nutrition. Both teams were successful.

Scientists determined that there was no way to make a viable gallon-sized paperboard carton. The side walls couldn't be made stiff enough, so the package bulged unacceptably. Besides, such a monster would be impossible for a child to handle and pour. The kitchens of America would be an inch deep in spilled milk from dropped gallon cartons! A brief experiment with a three-quart carton satisfied no one.

The team finally discovered that an inventor from Texas had developed a simple machine that applied a paper handle that securely fastened two half-gallon cartons together so they could be carried easily and, more important, priced and sold as one unit. After some testing and modification, the system was perfected and the new package configuration was christened the Gallon 2-Pak.

This looked like a good solution all around. The inexpensive machine could be installed easily at the end of dairy packaging lines. Supermarkets would be able to price the twin package as a gallon—that is, at a lower unit cost—while still protecting the extra margin they extracted from customers who only bought single half-gallons. And the new package could conceivably even offer benefits to the consumer. Only opening a half-gallon at a time kept the remaining milk fresher. Throwing away the carton when a half-gallon was gone freed space in the refrigerator, compared to that left by the gallon jug which took up the same amount of room no matter how little milk was left.

Meanwhile, IP's research team had uncovered something equally promising on the packaging and nutrition front. As far back as the 1940s, university scientists had observed that exposure to light had an effect on both the taste and vitamin content of milk. Study after study (77 were found, although a few were eventually rejected because of flawed methodology) showed that exposure to light produced an off-flavor in milk, or light-activated flavor, scientists called it. More important, light killed certain vitamins, principally vitamins A and B_2 (riboflavin). This observation had led years before to the use of metal milk boxes to protect the product when it was home-delivered in glass bottles, but the potential significance now was that milk in supermarket diary cases might be exposed to light 24 hours a day. Moreover, that light was fluorescent, which radiated the most damaging part of the spectrum. Further research determined that significant vitamin loss could be observed in as little as four hours, and that milk on average stayed in dairy cases several times that long. Furthermore, the vitamin loss was most pronounced in low-fat and skim milk, which the most health-conscious were buying.

New research proved that packaging did make a difference. Translucent plastic jugs permitted most of the light to pass through, while nearly opaque paperboard blocked out 94 percent of the harmful rays.

At last, the team had an issue to work with. The consumer buys milk because of its nutritional value. Milk packaged in plastic loses some of that nutritional value. Therefore, consumers who buy milk in paperboard cartons get more of what they buy milk for. The headlines almost wrote themselves.

Two critical questions remained, however. First, if the consumer learned this information, would she think it important enough to alter purchase behavior? Would it be a powerful enough motivation for the consumer to shop at a different store, to confront store management to demand milk in paper cartons, or even to pay more? And second, how could this complex story be communicated to the consumer clearly, and more important, credibly?

Research quickly supplied the answer to the first question: Yes, the consumer would alter behavior based on this information. Answers to the second question took a little longer to find. The search for answers was carried out by IP and its advertising agency using a method that had not yet been named—integrated marketing communications. The new process provided the appropriate framework for communicating with consumers.

Among the reasons for using an integrated marketing communications program were these:

Target audiences were multiple and diverse.

> Consumers wanted to keep their children healthy and to get value for their shopping dollars.

Dairies wanted to keep their supermarket customers happy and to keep their own costs down. Dairies also wanted consumers to buy more milk. (Per capita consumption had been declining in recent years.)

Supermarkets wanted to keep their regular shoppers happy and also to keep their own costs down.

There were several indirect audiences that needed to be enlisted as allies or neutralized.

Because milk is an important and highly regulated agricultural commodity, federal and state agencies ranging from the FDA to state milk boards could be expected to take an interest in the nutrition/packaging issue once it was opened.

Politicians at every level might be petitioned for information by voters or even asked to intercede by important contributors to their campaigns who saw their interests threatened—oil companies, for example, that supply the resin for plastic jugs.

Dairy and farm associations would be concerned about the effect of this program on the image of milk.

Security analysts who followed several interlocking industries—forest products, petroleum, the dairy industry, food retailing—would need to assess the potential impact, if any, of this communications program's success or failure.

It would be necessary to use multiple media.

The issue of paper cartons was not an "advertising" problem per se, instinct said and research proved. The subject was too important to the consumer, who perceived the nutritional value of milk as subconsciously related to her performance as a mother. Also, too much information was required before she could grasp the main point and the reasons why. And credibility was definitely an issue.

To clarify the packaging-nutrition issue, complementary but different messages would have to be communicated through dairy and grocery trade magazines.

The communications objective included not only brand awareness and trial, but altered beliefs that would lead to brand loyalty—all to be accomplished within a short time period.

At this point, DDB Needham's Keith Reinhard might ask, "What is the creative media concept?" What is the most effective method by which this particular message can be communicated to this particular consumer? When and where would the consumer seek information on this subject? Whom would she believe, and in what context? With this creative media concept at the center, what array of media can be used to repeat and reinforce the message; to lead the consumer to action; to reinforce the desired behavior; to make her not just a believer, but an advocate?

Consumer nutrition was the platform. Consumers were asked if they believe nutritional claims in advertising. Research suggested that the answer was, "Not entirely."

The consumer would be far more likely to believe a nutritional expert whom she perceived as objective, commenting in an editorial environment. Therefore, the decision was made to position the vitamin-loss-in-plastic issue first as a news story and then to use advertising to present paper cartons as a solution to the problem.

Ogilvy & Mather PR found an appropriate spokesperson, a young woman named Gail Levey. Ms. Levey was an accredited registered dietitian whose experience included both research and on-camera work for NBC on nutritional issues. After reviewing the 77 studies on the subject and consulting with various technical experts, she agreed to become the point person in the information phase of the International Paper's "consumer nutrition program", as the effort was now being called.

Over the next few months, while Ms. Levey became an authority on the subject of milk, light, and vitamins, Ogilvy & Mather PR prepared press kits and set up radio, television, and newspaper interviews for her in five test markets.

Meanwhile, development work proceeded on the advertising that would follow her appearances. The mix would include full-page newspaper ads using technical drawings and 1,500 words of factual copy to get across the basic story; a mother-and-child television commercial to inject the right emotional note and accelerate awareness; and radio spots (essentially the TV audio track) to increase exposure and multiply repetition. A question-and-answer format brochure written by Ms. Levey would be offered by mail to people who wanted more information.

While the consumer campaign was being developed by the agency, other parts of the task force worked on the trade program. The more-vitamins-to-the-gallon message responded to the core needs of the consumer, but reaching dairy and supermarket executives required a different strategy.

Supermarkets would have to offer milk in paperboard cartons in their dairy cases, of course, if consumers began to reject plastic. More than that, they would want to be on the right side of what could play out as a consumer affairs issue, not just as a question of personal preference or even of value.

Dairies, however, had a much bigger potential stake. A worrisome trend had developed during the previous decade. Per capita milk consumption had begun to decline. The task force decided to underscore the correlation between that decline and the shift to plastic. Could light-activated flavor—the off-taste produced by exposure to light—be a factor? This suggestion would be part of every communication to dairies, but the program itself was positioned as positive to milk, constantly reminding the consumer of milk's essential benefits for children, and thus potentially increasing milk consumption.

Sales presentations were created to enlist the cooperation of dairies and retailers in target markets. Dairies needed to be allies in the campaign to encourage supermarket participation and supermarkets needed not only to make more paper cartons available but also to help promote the concepts.

The promotional package included dairy brands and/or supermarket names in the consumer advertising; 25-cents-off coupons; co-op advertising allowances for both dairies and super-markets; large posters for supermarket windows; mobiles and shelf-talkers for point-of-purchase stimulation in the dairy aisle and dairy case; specially-printed side panels on milk cartons themselves, telling the more-vitamins story; even specially-printed grocery bags (which were also supplied by International Paper).

The sales presentation explained the purpose and extent of the effort, detailed the elements, and projected the expected result —a significant shift in consumer preference from plastic to paper.

Obviously, there was resistance from some dairies and supermarkets; however, most cooperated from the beginning, recognizing that the program would be perceived as being (and in fact was) in the consumers' interest.

The program rolled out in Sioux Falls, South Dakota, and never looked back.

Press coverage was extensive. Some newpapers used the more-vitamin story as food news; others treated it as consumer news. A few even picked it up as business news. Ms. Levey, an able performer, got significant time on radio and TV talk shows and additional exposure when several evening news teams decided that the story was interesting enough for feature treatment.

Buyer behavior changed almost immediately and acceler- ated when the advertising phased in two weeks later. Full-page ads listing stores where the Gallon 2-Pak was available and including a cents-off coupon ran on "best food day" in newspapers, in three-week flights, reinforced by 150 gross rating points (GRPs) per week of TV. Radio and point-of-purchase material increased exposure and maintained continuity between flights.

Tracking studies showed rapid increases in awareness and preference, with good understanding of the issue. Focus groups demonstrated the consumers' intensity of feelings on the subject. In-store intercepts indicated purchase intent. SAMI data proved altered behavior.

In market after market, the pattern was the same, and the results were similar. There was a shift from 59 percent/41 percent in favor of plastic to 65 percent/35 percent in favor of paper in Sioux Falls; from 61 percent/39 percent plastic to 57 percent/43 percent paper in Norfolk, Va.; a 27 percentage point gain for paper in San Diego; and a 35 point gain in Providence, R.I.; and total milk sales increased by an average of 10 percent.

Media modifications between test markets, accompanied by extensive qualitative and quantitative measurement, helped refine the program and improve efficiency. A media mix weighted too much toward broadcast increased awareness but reduced credibility and yielded lower (though still significant) behavior change. Reduced broadcast in favor of print reduced awareness to disappointing levels, though consumers exposed to the print messages were most likely to switch. Radio functioned well as a reminder medium, but could not substitute for television.

Trade advertising in grocery and dairy media was modified to include test market results and increase the sense of urgency and inevitability. A typical headline said "Consumer nutrition program increases milk sales 15 percent" and an overprinted line, timed by region, would say something like "Coming to your area October 15."

While International Paper had developed the program on its own, the Paperboard Packaging Council (PPC) had contributed funding to support the test market effort. Now the entire program was made available to other members of the PPC to run in sections of the country where different companies might have dominant market interests, and their subsequent experiences paralleled the earier test market results.

Ten years later, aseptic and hot-fill packaging and other higher-value end uses have absorbed part of the bleached board capacity once dedicated to milk cartons, but paper continues to hold a significant share of the milk packaging market. The consumer nutrition message is well-understood and still acted on by a significant number of milk-buying consumers, and various elements of the program are still run by companies in various parts of the country.

The total profit impact of this integrated marketing communications program on paperboard packaging producers during the decade of the '80s was several times the total investment.

Experts within the industry and outside observers alike agree key reasons for this success include:

> the focus from the beginning on finding a solution to a business problem, not on developing an ad campaign;

the absence of artificial deadlines, such as a date advertising would have to begin;

inclusion in the planning process of everyone who might have something to contribute, both from the company side and from the agencies;

acceptance by all parties of accountability for results;

thorough research to determine the distinct roles and motivations of each target audience segment, from the consumer back through each intermediate distribution step;

single-minded but coherently arrayed message selection based on the needs and wants of each separate "receiver;"

mission-minded media selection based on effectiveness criteria such as credibility and function, not just efficiency;

total integration from the planning process forward of all communication elements, including consumer and trade advertising, PR, direct marketing, promotion, and presentations;

close cooperation from problem definition through solution development and implementation by all parties to the business process, including strategic planners, researchers, and product developers on the company side, several kinds of functional expertise on the agency side, outside research firms with various specialities, and legal counsel.

In an earlier era, the response to a business problem like this might have been, "Let's run some ads." (In too many companies today, this still may be the *modus operandi*.) The ads would have been developed to say what the company wanted to say, usually something about the product, rather than to address a consumer's genuine needs. Other activities would have been considered supporting activities, called "collateral," and developed after the fact. The results would have been negligible to nonexistent—as in fact they were in earlier attempts to solve this same problem. Nor would anyone have been held accountable.

The integrated marketing communications process begins with a business problem, does not assume an advertising solution, takes the time necessary to research and develop an integrated strategy, puts all elements in place before pulling the trigger, measures everything, and accepts accountability.

These are the new criteria of business success—if not survival—as the millennium dawns.

Index

AARP (Association for the
    Advancement of Retired
    People), 10
Accountability, 15, 99
Accountability-based
    compensation system, 101.
    See also Compensation
    systems
    of DDB Needham, 102–103
Accumulation model, 41–42,
    46–47
Advertising
    and integration, 13–16
    in 1950s–1960s, 5–6
    and receiver, 7
    after World War II, 4
Advertising agency, in 1970s,
    6–8
Affiliations, 142–143
Agency relationship manager, 168
American Association of Retired
    Persons (AARP), 143
American Cancer Society (ACS),
    IMC in, 180–196
American Medical Association,
    planning model and, 59, 61
Analysis, of consumer response
    data, 125
Anderson, Arthur, 104
Attitudes, 119
    formation of, 108

Barriers
    to IMC, 157–179
    organizational structure as,
        160–174
    overcoming, 177–179
Bateman, Thomas S., 25
Behavior, 108. *See also*
    Purchases
    attitudes as, 119
    database, and measurement of,
        107
    forms of, 117
    multidimensional measures of,
        116–117
    technology and measurement of,
        111–112
Bellow, Saul, 6
Benefits
    competitive, 76–78
    of Nike, 78–80
Beverage hierarchy illustration,
    35
Brand-focused structure, 169
Brand management organization,
    162, 163
    revisions to, 172–174
Brand networks
    hierarchy concept and,
        126–127
    information storage and, 47–51
    measurement and, 121,
        125–127

Brand parity, 65
Brands
  contact inventories and,
    132–133
  contact paths and, 133–138
  personality of, 80–81
  selling idea for, 89–91
Budgets. *See* Compensation
Budweiser, selling idea for, 95, 96
Business-to-business marketer,
    planning model and, 59, 60
Buying incentive. *See* Target
    Buying Incentive

Cable television, 10
Campbell, 101
Cancer, media campaign about,
    180–196
Capture-enhance-update systems,
    124
Cashless society, 150
Catalogs
  marketers of, 124–125
  organizations, 147
Category and brand networks,
    47–51
Centralized management control,
    165–168
Change, resistance to, 157–158
Chiat/Day, 14
Chunking, 36–37
Circular marketing
    communications programs,
    152–154
Client-agency relationship, and
    compensation, 99
Commission marketers, and
    incentive systems, 101–102
Commitment measures, 121,
    140–146
Communication
  and action objectives, 81–82
  centralized, 178–179
  changes in, 18–23
  as competitive advantage, 178
  controllable and
    uncontrollable, 115
  and functional illiteracy, 20–21
  and information processing,
    24–26
  logistics and, 44
  marketing messages and,
    29–32

in marketing organizations,
    162–163
one-way to two-way, 51–52
perceptions, facts, and 22–23
in processing system, 27–28
stimulus-response model of,
    27–28
strategy for, 57
and two-way information flow,
    124
verbal to visual, 19–20
Communication effects model,
    110–111, 117
Communications. *See also*
    Marketing communications
Communications central
    authority, 165–168
Communications measurement
  circular model of, 112–113
  IMC view of, 111–114
Communications mix, 68
Communications program,
    strategy of, 64–86
Communications strategy, to
    execution, 87–98
Compensation systems, 99–106
  drivers of, 106
  fees, performance, and,
    103–105
  and Guaranteed Results,
    102–103
  incentive systems, 101–102
  resource-based fee systems,
    102–106
Competition, knowing, 75–76
Competitive benefit, 76–78
Competitive brand positioning,
    68
Complex channels, measuring
    purchases through, 148–152
Computers, 11, 19–20
Concepts. *See also* Information
    processing; Judgment
  creation and storage of, 26
  as networks, 35, 36–37
  storage of information about,
    47–51
Consumable products, tracking,
    148–152
Consumer behavior. *See*
    Behavior
Consumer commitment,
    140–146

external measures of, 142–143
internal measures of, 144–146
Consumer contacts, as
    communication device,
    123–124
Consumer hierarchy, 47–51. *See
    also* Information processing
Consumer nutrition, 204–205
Consumer responses, measuring,
    123–156
Consumers, 11, 12–13. *See also*
    Behavior; Stimulus-response
    model
    contact measurement and, 121,
    132–140
    decoding marketing messages
    by, 30–32
    measuring product contact of,
    138–140
    perceptions, facts and, 22–23
Contact management, 56–57
Contact measures. *See* Contacts,
    measurement of
Contact points, customer, 83
Contacts
    with brands, 51
    inventories of, 132–133
    mapping of, 133–138
    measurement of, 121,
    123–124, 132–140
    paths of, 133–138
Cost reduction, 11–12
Creative process, 87–98
    and creative person, 88–89
    selling ideas and, 89–98
Credit card organizations, 124
Credit information, 146
Customer-focused marketing,
    178
Customer purchase
    measurement, 146–154

Dairy marketing, 197–209
Database
    and IMC planning model,
    55–58
    responses to, 124–125
    and two-way relationship
    communications systems,
    52–53
    users of, 55
Database analysis, 107–114
Database marketing, 146–147

cost of, 176–177
Data overlays, 142
DDB Needham, 14, 187–189,
    204
    and Guaranteed Results
    system, 102–103
Debit systems, 150
Demassification, 6–8
Diary information, 149
Digital delivery, 155–156
Direct mail organizations, 147
Direct marketers, 55
Direct marketing program, 67
Direct purchase measurement,
    146
Distribution, 12
Drucker, Peter, 1, 14, 159, 178

Economies of scale, 11–12
Efficiency experts, 4
800 numbers, 144
Electronic data capture, 149–150
Electronic data delivery, 155
Electronic funds transfers, 150
Empowerment, 8–10
Execution strategy, 69
Expanded response measure, 120
Experiences, fields of, 28
External consumer commitment
    measures, 142–143

Facts, perceptions and, 22–23
First Team, The, 14
FOCUS theory, 6–7
Ford, Henry, 6
Four Ps theory, 5, 12
Functional illiteracy, 20–21
Functional specialists, 164
Future Shock, 6

Gallup, George, 7
General Electric, FOCUS theory
    of, 6–7
Goals, 81–82
Government organization,
    planning model and, 63
Guaranteed Results
    compensation system,
    102–103
Gutman, 128

Hierarchical storage. *See*
Information processing;
Storage
Hierarchy of effects model,
108–109
and measurement, 126–127
Horizontal structure, 163–164
Howard, John, 128

IBM contact map, 134–137
Illiteracy, functional, 20–21
Imagination, capturing, 87–98
IMC. *See* Integrated marketing
communications
IMC planning model, 161
and American Cancer Society,
188
Incentive systems, 101–102
Indirect purchase measurement,
147–148
Information. *See also*
Communication
analysis of incoming, 125
control of, 38
data overlays, 142
overload, 39
two-way flow of, 124
Information explosion, 38
Information processing, 24–26,
32–36, 38–40, 47–51
application of, 43–63
model of, 33
Information Resources, Inc. (IRI),
150–152
Information storage, 22
and attitudes, 119
Information storage systems, in
human mind, 32–36
Inside-out planning model,
159–160
Integrated marketing
communications
and American Cancer Society,
180–196
circular nature of, 58–59
differences with traditional
marketing, 55–56
history of, 1–16
measuring, 114–122
new measures in, 116
and paperboard milk cartons,
198–209
planning model, 54, 55–63

Integrated marketing program,
developing, 43–63
Integrated Systems Data
Networks (ISDN), 155
Integration, 13–16
Internal consumer commitment
measures, 144–146
Internal relationship manager,
167–168
Internal Revenue Service,
planning model and, 62, 63
International Paper, 198–209
Interpersonal communication
model, 27–28
Inventories, of contacts, 132–133
ISDN. *See* Integrated Systems
Data Network

Judgment, 34–36
consumer system, 31–32

Kellogg's, selling idea for, 90, 91,
92

Laddering, 127–129
Land's End catalog, 147
Lauterborn, Robert, 12
Lavidge, Robert J., 108
Levey, Gail, 204–205
Levitt, Ted, 6, 15
Logistics, and communication, 44
Long-term store (LTS), 34
LTS. *See* Long-term store

Magazines, 10
Manufacturing man, 3–4
Mapping
contact, 133–138
MDS, 130
Marcom department, 99–101
Marcom manager, 165–167
Market-focused structure,
169-172
Marketing. *See also* Integrated
marketing communications
campaign planning and, 153
changes in, 11–13
consumer perception of, 45
mass, 5–6
message sending and, 29–31
and 1990s, 8–10
objectives of, 57
relationship, 39–40, 52

tools of, 58
traditional, 45–46, 55–56
trends in, 10–13
Marketing communications
    continuum of, 46
    department. *See* Marcom
        department
    functioning of, 17–42
    operation of, 29–32
    tactics, 58
Marketing communications
    measurement, traditional,
    functional approaches to,
    110–111
Marketing department. *See*
    Marcom department
Marketing integration, 13–16
Marketing mix, 43
Marketing Myopia, 6, 15
Marketing operations, 173
    services/communications,
    173–174
Marketing organizations. *See also*
    Organizational structure
    capability of, 174–175
    and database marketing, 176
    and marketplace information,
    175–176
Marketing
    services/communications,
    173–174
Market research, types of, 142
Market segment management,
    169–172
Mass marketing, 5–6
Mass media, collapse of, 10
MDS. *See* Multidimensional
    scaling
Measurement. *See also*
    Communications
    measurement; Research
    of behavior, 108–114
    of contacts, 132–140
    and database analysis,
    107–114
    digital delivery, ISDN, and, 155
    of integrated marketing
        communications, 114–122
    laddering and, 127–129
    of marketing program,
    107–122
    of responses, 123–156
    tracking studies and, 138–139

transactional programs for,
    154–155
types of, 120–122
Media. *See also* Mass media
    mergers of, 15
    1950s–1960s, 5–6
    in 1990s, 10
    in World War II, 2–4
Media campaign, of public service
        organization. *See* American
        Cancer Society
Media fragmentation, 21–22
Megatrends, 7
Mental network. *See* Networks
Message, 57
    accumulation model of, 41–42
    marketers' sending of, 29–32
    replacement model of, 40–41
Message delivery, 108
Meyers-Levy, Joan, 35, 51
Milk cartons. *See* Paperboard
    milk cartons
Models. *See* models by name
Modern Maturity, 10
Morgan, Lee Anne, 103, 105–106
Morgan Anderson & Company
    (MAC), resource-based fee
    system of, 103–106
MRI, 53
Multidimensional
    communications
    measurement, 116–117
Multidimensional scaling,
    129–131
Munro, Dick, 15

Naisbitt, John, 7–8
Networks, 46–47
    brand, 125–127
    category and brand, 47–51
    concepts as, 36, 37
    measurement of change in, 121
New Age consumers, 12–13
New Realities, The, 1
Nike, campaign of, 78–80
900 numbers, 144
Nissan, selling idea for, 94–95
Non-profit
    companies/associations,
    planning model and, 59, 61
Nutrition, and paperboard
    marketing, 204–205

Ogilvy & Mather, 200
Ogilvy, David, 15
One-way communications, 51–52
Organ, Dennis W., 25
Organizational change, resistance
    to, 157–158
Organizational structure
    and communications central
        authority, 165–168
    functional specialists and, 164
    horizontal, 163–164
    as IMC barrier, 160–174
    restructuring and, 169–172
    vertical, 163–164

Packaged goods companies, and
    incentive systems, 101–102
Packaging. *See* Paperboard milk
    cartons
Paperboard milk cartons,
    198–209
Paperboard Packaging Council
    (PPC), 197, 207
Perception, 24–26
    change in, 82–83
    and facts, 22–23
    model of process, 25
    of product, 74–75
Performance. *See* Compensation
Personal communication, 64
Personality, of message, 80–81
Planning systems, 158–160
    inside-out, 159–160
Population, aging of, 10
Porche, selling idea for, 92–94
Positioning theory, 7
Pre-post tests, 131–132
Pricing, 68
Print, 10
Processing, of communications
    messages, 27–28
Product
    perception of, 74–75
    reality of, 73–74
    reason to believe in, 78
Product affiliations, as
    relationships, 118–119
Product management systems,
    163
Promotion, measuring, 148–152.
    See also American Cancer
    Society; Paperboard milk
    cartons

Promotions, 67
Propaganda campaign, 2–3
Prospects, 145
Public service organization,
    media campaign of. *See*
    American Cancer Society
Purchase behavior, 111–112. *See
    also* Behavior; Measurement
Purchasers, measures of, 122
Purchases
    measuring, 146–154
    as transactions, 117–119

Receiver, of advertising, 7
Reinhard, Keith, 14–15, 204
Relationship manager, 167–168
Relationship marketing, 52,
    39–40
Relationships, 118–119
Remuneration systems, and
    incentive systems, 101–102
Replacement model, 40–41
Research. *See also* Market
    research; Measurement
    laddering and, 127–129
    multidimensional scaling and,
        129–131
    and pre-post tests, 131–132
Research studies, syndicated, 53
Resource-based fee systems,
    103–106
Response coupon, 144
Responses
    capturing, 140
    generating, 144
    measurement of, 123–156
    solicitation of, 124
Retailers, 12, 149–150
Retraining, 15–16
Reynolds, 128
Ries, Al, 6
Roberts, Donald, 27

Saatchi & Saatchi, 14
Sales, 173
Scanner panel data, 148, 151
Schramm, Wilbur, 27
Schultz, Don E., 29
Search firms, 100–101
Segmentation process, 57
Selling, 64. *See also* Strategy
Selling idea, 89–91
    outstanding, 97–98

source of, 91–95, 96
Sensory register (SR), 33–34
Service, selling idea for, 89–91
Service cards, 147–148
Shopper panel, 149
Short-term memory store (STS), 34
Simmons, 53
Simmons Market Research Bureau, 200
Skin cancer, media campaign about, 180–196
Statistical analysis procedures, 125
Steiner, Gary A., 108
Stimulus-response model, 27–28
Storage, information, 33–36, 47–51
Strategy
  action goals and, 81–82
  of communications program, 64–86
  to execution, 87–98
  future and, 84–85
  outline of, 85–86
  perceptual change and, 82–83
  types of, 69
Syndicated data, 149
Syndicated studies, 53, 142

Tactics, 58
Tannenbaum, Stanley I., 29
Target audiences, and paperboard cartons, 102–104
Target Buying Incentive (TBI), 70–73
TBI. See Target Buying Incentive
Technology, 43–44
  and behavior measurement, 111–112

and media fragmentation, 21–22
Telecommunications company structure, 165–167
Telephone numbers, 800 and 900, 144
Television, 10
Time, measurements over, 116
Time-Warner, 15
Toffler, Alvin, 6
Toll-free numbers, 144
Tonality, of message, 80–81
Tools, 58
Tracking studies, 138–139
Transactional programs, 154–155
Transactions, 117–118
  partial, 118
  process of, 111–112
Trend Reports, 7
Trends, 10–13
Trout, Jack, 6
Two-way communications, 51–52
  database and, 52–53
Two-way marketing, 146
Tybout, Alice M., 35, 51, 128

Universal Product Code (UPC), 149

Verbal communications, 19–20
Vertical structure, 163–164
Video, 10
Visual communications, 19–20

Wanamaker, John, 4
Warranty cards, 140, 147–148
World War II, and marketing, 2–3

About the Authors

▼

Don E. Schultz is Professor of Advertising and Integrated Marketing Communications at the Medill School of Journalism, Northwestern University, where he and his associates have pioneered the country's first graduate program in Integrated Marketing Communications. He is also President of his own marketing communications and management firm, Agora, Inc., Evanston, Illinois.

Before joining Northwestern in 1977, Schultz was Senior Vice President of Tracy-Locke Advertising and Public Relations in Dallas. He has consulted, lectured and held seminars on marketing, marketing communications, advertising, sales promotion, direct marketing and creative strategy in the United States, Europe, South America and Asia.

Schultz is Editor, *Journal of Direct Marketing*, Director of the Promotion Marketing Association of America, and the first recipient of the Direct Marketing Educator of the Year Award, presented by the Direct Marketing Educational Foundation.

Stanley Tannenbaum joined Northwestern University as Associate Professor in the Medill School of Journalism in 1983 and he now holds the Chair of the Advertising/Integrated Marketing Communications Division.

Tannenbaum started in advertising as a copywriter at a small package goods agency in Philadelphia, working on the introduction of Alpo Dog Food. He then went to RCA as a writer in charge of Sales Promotion, Cooperative Advertising and Public

Relations. From RCA, he moved to Kenyon & Eckhardt in New York, an international advertising agency, where he rose from copywriter to Chairman of the Board. After 26 years at K&E, he joined his client, Turtle Wax, as Executive Vice President.

Tannenbaum has served on the Board of the Association of American Advertising Agencies, the Advertising Council, and the National Advertising Review Board.

Robert F. Lauterborn is the James L. Knight Professor of Advertising in the School of Journalism and Mass Communication at the University of North Carolina at Chapel Hill.

For ten years prior to this appointment, Lauterborn was director of marketing communication and corporate advertising for international Paper Company. Before joining IP, he spent 16 years with General Electric in various industrial and corporate positions.

Currently, Lauterborn is a principal of Morgan, Anderson & Company, a leading marketing communications management consulting firm. He has served on the boards of many professional organizations, including the ANA, ARF, B/PAA, AAF, BPA, CBBB, NARB, and several companies.

TITLES OF INTEREST IN MARKETING, DIRECT MARKETING, AND SALES PROMOTION

SUCCESSFUL DIRECT MARKETING METHODS, Fourth Edition, by Bob Stone
PROFITABLE DIRECT MARKETING, Second Edition, by Jim Kobs
CREATIVE STRATEGY IN DIRECT MARKETING, by Susan K. Jones
READINGS AND CASES IN DIRECT MARKETING, by Herb Brown and Bruce Buskirk
STRATEGIC DATABASE MARKETING, by Robert R. Jackson and Paul Wang
SUCCESSFUL TELEMARKETING, Second Edition, by Bob Stone and John Wyman
BUSINESS TO BUSINESS DIRECT MARKETING, by Robert Bly
INTEGRATED MARKETING COMMUNICATIONS, by Don E. Schultz, Stanley I. Tannenbaum, and Robert F. Lauterborn
NEW DIRECTIONS IN MARKETING, by Aubrey Wilson
GREEN MARKETING, by Jacquelyn Ottman
MARKETING CORPORATE IMAGE: THE COMPANY AS YOUR NUMBER ONE PRODUCT, by James R. Gregory with Jack G. Wiechmann
HOW TO CREATE SUCCESSFUL CATALOGS, by Maxwell Sroge
SALES PROMOTION ESSENTIALS, Second Edition, by Don E. Schultz, William A. Robinson and Lisa Petrison
PROMOTIONAL MARKETING: IDEAS AND TECHNIQUES FOR SUCCESS IN SALES PROMOTION, by William A. Robinson and Christine Hauri
BEST SALES PROMOTIONS, Sixth Edition, by William A. Robinson
INSIDE THE LEADING MAIL ORDER HOUSES, Third Edition, by Maxwell Sroge
NEW PRODUCT DEVELOPMENT, Second Edition, by George Gruenwald
NEW PRODUCT DEVELOPMENT CHECKLISTS, by George Gruenwald
CLASSIC FAILURES IN PRODUCT MARKETING, by Donald W. Hendon
THE COMPLETE TRAVEL MARKETING HANDBOOK, by Andrew Vladimir
HOW TO TURN CUSTOMER SERVICE INTO CUSTOMER SALES, by Bernard Katz
THE MARKETING PLAN, by Robert K. Skacel
ADVERTISING & MARKETING CHECKLISTS, by Ron Kaatz
SECRETS OF SUCCESSFUL DIRECT MAIL, by Richard V. Benson
U.S. DEPARTMENT OF COMMERCE GUIDE TO EXPORTING
HOW TO GET PEOPLE TO DO THINGS YOUR WAY, by J. Robert Parkinson
THE 1-DAY MARKETING PLAN, by Roman A. Hiebing, Jr. and Scott W. Cooper
HOW TO WRITE A SUCCESSFUL MARKETING PLAN, by Roman G. Hiebing, Jr. and Scott W. Cooper
DEVELOPING, IMPLEMENTING, AND MANAGING EFFECTIVE MARKETING PLANS, by Hal Goetsch
HOW TO EVALUATE AND IMPROVE YOUR MARKETING DEPARTMENT, by Keith Sparling and Gerard Earls
SELLING TO A SEGMENTED MARKET, by Chester A. Swenson
MARKET-ORIENTED PRICING, by Michael Morris and Gene Morris
STATE-OF-THE-ART MARKETING RESEARCH, by A.B. Blankenship and George E. Breen
WAS THERE A PEPSI GENERATION BEFORE PEPSI DISCOVERED IT?, by Stanley C. Hollander and Richard Germain
BUSINESS TO BUSINESS COMMUNICATIONS HANDBOOK, by Fred Messner
SALES LEADS: HOW TO CONVERT EVERY PROSPECT INTO A CUSTOMER, by Robert Donath, James Obermeyer, Carol Dixon and Richard Crocker
AMA MARKETING TOOLBOX (SERIES), by David Palmerlee & Allan Sutherlin
AMA COMPLETE GUIDE TO SMALL BUSINESS MARKETING, by Ken Cook
101 TIPS FOR MORE PROFITABLE CATALOGS, by Maxwell Sroge
HOW TO GET THE MOST OUT OF TRADE SHOWS, by Steve Miller
HOW TO GET THE MOST OUT OF SALES MEETINGS, by James Dance
MARKETING TO CHINA, by Xu Bai Yi
STRATEGIC MARKET PLANNING, by Robert J. Hamper and L. Sue Baugh
COMMONSENSE DIRECT MARKETING, Second Edition, by Drayton Bird
NTC'S DICTIONARY OF DIRECT MAIL AND MAILING LIST TERMINOLOGY AND TECHNIQUES, by Nat G. Bodian

 For further information or a current catalog, write:
NTC Business Books
a division of *NTC Publishing Group*
4255 West Touhy Avenue
Lincolnwood, Illinois 60646-1975 U.S.A.